Slips of the Ear

Slips of the Ear

Errors in the Perception of Casual Conversation

Zinny S. Bond

Department of Linguistics
Ohio University
Athens, Ohio

With a Foreword by Anne Cutler

Cover photo: Christoph Wilhelm/FPG

P
37.5
.S67
B66
1999

Academic Press
A Harcourt Science and Technology Company
525 B Street, Suite 1900, San Diego, California 92101-4495, USA
http://www.academicpress.com

Academic Press Limited
24-28 Oval Road, London NW1 7DX
http://www.hbuk.co.uk/ap/

Library of Congress Catalog Card Number: 99-65866

International Standard Book Number 0-12-113340-0

PRINTED IN THE UNITED STATES OF AMERICA

99   00   01   02   03   04   MM   9   8   7   6   5   4   3   2   1

In memory of my parents,
Marija Didrichson Sans and Rudolf Sans

Kas var zvaigznes izskaitīt?
Kas valodu izrunāt?

Who can count all the stars?
Who can use up language?
  —Latvian folk song

CONTENTS

FOREWORD

Listening to speech is one of the most refined skills that we humans have. It is a skill which is exquisitely tailored to the native language; this happens during the first year of life, even before the little listener has become a little speaker. It is an extraordinarily robust skill. As listeners we have no problem understanding speakers whose voices we have never heard before. We can understand men and women and children though their vocal apparatus will produce enormously different acoustic signals. We can comprehend speech against considerable background noise, and we can compensate for the effects of arbitrary blockages of the vocal tract such as a cold in the nose, a pipe clenched between the teeth, or a mouthful of food. The radical bandpass restrictions imposed by communications systems do not prevent us from conversing on the telephone. Listening to our native language seems simple and virtually effortless.

But the impression of simplicity covers a highly complex perceptual performance. Although to listeners it seems as if speakers utter one word after another, in fact speakers do not make it particularly easy for listeners to apprehend words in sequence. Speech signals are produced as a continuous stream, and they contain no consistent and obvious cues—except perhaps at the boundaries of larger syntactic units—to inform the listener where one word ends and the next begins. There are, furthermore, far-reaching contextual effects of phonemes upon one another, so that simple invariant cues to phoneme identity can also not be counted upon. Listeners have to decode the speech signal to extract from it the discrete words which the speaker originally encoded. It is, after all, the words which form the common knowledge base upon which speakers and listeners draw. Each utterance may be entirely new, but it should be made up of words which both parties to spoken interaction know. Recognition of an utterance as the sequence of individual words which compose it constitutes quite a feat, given the continuity and the contextual variability of speech; nevertheless, it is a feat which we perform with heedless ease.

Only very occasionally does the process go wrong. It is perhaps remarkable that this book is not enormously larger. Slips of the ear do not happen regularly, every few listening minutes, as a matter of routine. Why not, given the complexity of the listening task? The struggle to answer this question has kept speech scientists and psycholinguists busy for generations. The answer draws, as one would expect given the robustness of human listening, on the flexibility of our perceptual system. This system is, one might say, "overengineered": it is full of backup and fail-safe features. Indecision or inadequacy at one processing level can be resolved or compensated for at another level. The comprehension system is not a fragile chain that is only as strong as its weakest link; it is more like a well-practiced team where any member may be called upon to deliver greater or lesser performance in a given operation. When the process does then go wrong, it is because the team as a whole has been unable to complete the task, not because one element has fallen short.

It follows from this that when slips of the ear do occur, they provide researchers with data about the way the team performs, i.e., about the comprehension system as a whole. Thus when a listener reports hearing "oregano nose" in place of "a ring in her nose," the implications are not confined to the fact that a higher front vowel may be misperceived as a mid front vowel, and a velar nasal as a velar stop; experiments in perceptual confusion, and indeed comparison of acoustic signals, could already have led us to expect that. The error allows us the further insight that the comprehension system does not necessarily prevent such a misperception from gaining access to conscious awareness. A listener who hears "you can spend a minute" when the speaker actually said "you can spend a mint" provides us information about more than the evidence requirements for the perception of weak vowels in English; the error also sheds light on listeners' choices between sequences of greater or lesser transitional probability. This is also true, of course, of the listener who hears the nonword "chine" for "chain," since the probability of nonwords occurring in casual conversation is very low!

The architecture of the human language processing system is a subject of heated psycholinguistic debate centered on the following issue: are levels of language processing autonomous, or is there feedback from later stages of processing to logically prior stages? Evidence of how likely listeners are to perceive nonwords, or of the relative proportions of high- and low-frequency words in reported misperceptions, can shed light on this issue, just as can listeners' ability to appreciate puns or to notice when speakers make slips of the tongue.

Thus we can ask many sorts of questions about the wealth of material in this volume. How often do these various types of error occur? Do errors differ greatly, or are there clear patterns to be found? To some of these questions, the book provides answers. But more importantly, it provides the means for us to find out for ourselves the answers to new questions. It cannot offer ready-made answers to all the research questions about slips of the ear, because many such questions may yet be devised. When future researchers construct hypotheses from which predictions about perceptual errors in listening can be derived, however, the predictions may be tested against this corpus. The errors in the corpus come almost exclusively from "causal conversations"—that is, from real life. All large corpora with potential relevance to theory are useful; but corpora of naturally occurring real-life data, because of the great investment of effort in the collection process which they represent, are rare and particularly valuable. There is no misunderstanding that!

Anne Cutler

PREFACE

When we are trying to understand a phenomenon, it makes sense to look at it in its natural habitat. This work is about speakers and listeners engaging in what they do every day, talking to each other in all sorts of circumstances about all sorts of topics. In doing this, speakers and listeners employ knowledge of their language with no effort or conscious attention. Most of the time, the results appear flawless in that speakers produce utterances as they intend and listeners understand them. Sometimes some part of the process goes wrong. Sometimes speakers make errors in production and listeners make errors in perception, hearing something which does not correspond to a speaker's utterance. Errors are part of the natural history of language use. Errors in the perception and understanding of utterances are the topic of this project.

When we look at errors in perception, we find that listeners are constrained by the sounds of language, on the one hand, and by the desire to make sense of what they hear, on the other. They use knowledge of their language to bridge this gap.

Over the years, many people have contributed to this project. I want to thank all my colleagues, friends, and students who have supplied examples of misperceptions to add to the data set. Without their kindness and assistance, this project would have been impossible. In particular, I want to acknowledge Joann Fokes, Sara Garnes, Ilse Lehiste, Danny Moates, Randall Robey, Larry Small, Verna Stockmal, and Robert Watkins.

A portion of this project was supported by a Faculty Fellowship from Ohio University. Portions of this project were supported by AFOSR.

Zinny S. Bond

CHAPTER 1

Introduction

Under normal every-day conditions all phonetic input must be considered potentially . . . indeterminate.
                                                    —Bernd Voss (1984)

1.1. INTRODUCTORY REMARKS

Even though the phonetic information supplied to them by a speaker is variously ambiguous, degraded, or unclear, linguistically sophisticated listeners are rarely misled. Listeners who know a language also know speech-understanding strategies which enable them to recover an intended message rapidly and accurately.

On occasion, however, listeners' strategies for dealing with speech lead them into an erroneous perception of the intended message—a misperception, or a slip of the ear. A listener reports hearing, as clearly and distinctly as any correctly perceived stretch of speech, something that does not correspond to the speaker's actual utterance. These errors in perception provide unique insight into the speech perception strategies used under normal everyday circumstances.

Misperceptions are the topic of this study. Its goal is to provide a description and classification of all errors available in my collection at Ohio University. Some properties of the misperceptions in this data set have been reported previously in a number of publications (Bond, 1973; Garnes & Bond, 1975; Bond & Garnes, 1980a, 1980b; Bond & Robey, 1983). Providing a description of the corpus of perceptual errors is motivated by continuing interest in speech perception, speech understanding, and the ways they can go astray. It also is motivated by an observation made by Norman (1981, p. 13) in his analysis of errors in actions:

> The collection and analysis of naturally occurring errors forces us to consider behavior that is not constrained by the limitations and artificiality of the experimental laboratory. By examining errors, we are forced to demonstrate that our theoretical ideas can have some relevance to real behavior.

Theories of speech perception and speech understanding can profit by being sensitive to the characteristics of naturally occurring slips of the ear. Ultimately, of course, "to validate what has been theoretically postulated as the cause of errors, laboratory tests are useful" (Norman, 1981, p. 14). Slips of the ear provide a natural field of observation against which theoretical constructs in linguistics and psychology can be tested.

1.2. THE DATA SET

All the examples of misperceptions have been gathered from ordinary conversational speech. Some errors were obtained while I participated as either a speaker or listener in a conversation during which a misperception occurred; others have been noted by observation of a misperception, detectable because the listener asked for clarification from the speaker. A sizable number of such examples have been reported by interested students, friends, and colleagues. The data, therefore, consist of anecdotal reports gathered over a period of years. Clearly, the data set has been created through an uncontrolled sampling procedure. The corpus of perceptual errors undoubtedly leans toward the more obvious or noticeable, errors which were significant enough to make listeners puzzled about what they heard. The errors which were reported are also probably the most memorable.

The data set for this report consists of almost 900 tokens of misperceptions, the entire collection limited only to the analysis to misperceptions found in English conversations. As a practical matter, errors have been classified into separate types: simple vowel misperceptions, simple consonant misperceptions, and multiple complex misperceptions. Simple errors reside in one segment of one word, whether a vowel or a consonant. For example, the perceptual error

Jim's out with his van → with his fan

represents a simple consonant error; only the initial consonant of the word *van* was misperceived. Each of the misperceptions in the two examples

heart-to-heart → hard-to-hard
kills germs where they grow → kills germs with egg roll

are not simple according to this definition, in that the first misperception involves more than one word and the second involves a complex set of consonant misperceptions. Though the data are presented separately for simple phonetic errors vs. multiple complex errors, this classification is for convenience rather than being based on any theoretical considerations.

Approximately one-third of the data set consisted of simple misperceptions affecting consonants; two-thirds were complex misperceptions. There were less than 50 errors affecting only vowels. In addition, a number of misperceptions seemed to involve extreme restructuring of the target utterance. These are listed in Chapter 7. The errors are primarily representative of adults. Just over 100 of the observed errors were contributed by children.

The vast majority of errors occurred in face-to-face conversations. The details of the conversational situations varied considerably, as is characteristic of much incidental speech. For instance, some misperceptions occurred in a car, or while the conversers were working on a project of some sort, eating a meal, or ordering food in a restaurant. In essence, the face-to-face errors occurred while people were conducting ordinary daily life. Telephone conversations accounted for only 2% of the errors. Approximately 5% of the errors occurred in a listening situation in which the speaker was addressing the listener indirectly, e.g., via radio, television, or a public address system. Information concerning the social or regional dialects of participants in conversations was available only very rarely. Of the total set of misperceptions, approximately 21% involved a proper name in some way. Although it is not clear what percentage one ought to expect, the percent of proper names seems high. The percentage may reflect the fact that proper names are less constrained by phonology and expectation than are ordinary lexical items.

1.3. DATA CODING AND ANALYSIS

Each error was entered in a computer file along with classification codes. The data analysis was performed by means of a program written in REXX. Vowel errors were classified according to the nature of the misperceived syllable, whether stressed or unstressed. The intended (target) and misperceived vowels were further classified according to the dimensions of the traditional vowel quadrilateral, as front, central, back; high, mid, low; and tense, lax. The nonphonemic diphthongs /e/ and /o/ were treated as vowels. Intended and perceived consonants were classified according to the traditional place, manner, and voicing categories. Consonants appearing in clusters were treated separately from consonants appearing as singletons. Complex errors were classified for consonant and vowel misperceptions—that is, for loss, addition, or substitution, as well as for changes in word boundaries, syllable number, and stress pattern. In addition, all tokens of misperceptions were coded for their occurrence in proper names, for changes in the order of syllables or segments, and for the occurrence of phonetic sequences which are not words in English, i.e., nonsense words.

Inevitably, any classification scheme involves some arbitrary decisions; the relatively simple scheme employed here is no exception. Accurate phonetic representations of the speakers' utterances were never available. Consequently, the nature of target utterances is ultimately an assumption. By convention, all targets were assumed to have a relatively distinct pronunciation, on the grounds that such a representation best captures the speaker's intent. In the case of words which are habitually reduced in conversational speech, such as *and,* assuming a distinct vowel /æ/ is certainly an arbitrary and perhaps unrealistic decision, yet it is true of the speaker's intention to communicate the word *and.* By assuming that a distinct pronunciation served as a target, however, the onus for misperceptions was placed on the listener, not necessarily correctly.

Word boundary placements were traditional; all but clearly contracted function words were treated as separate lexical items. In the case of spoken sequences of alphabetical characters, as in the misperception

He's an ENT → an E and T,

each spoken character was treated as a separate lexical item. Constructions with function words, such as a verb followed by a particle as well as derived nouns (e.g., *drive-in*), were treated as separate lexical items. Numerical constructions such as *four nation* and *sixty-seven* were also treated as two words. Speakers were assumed to be employing the most expected stress patterns for any utterance. The distinction between proper names and common nouns was made on a case-by-case basis. *American* was a name; *Fourier* in *Fourier analysis* was not. Decisions whether an error involved omissions, substitutions, or reorderings were conservative, favoring omissions and substitutions.

A further difficulty involves the exact nature of the misperception. When a listener misunderstands or misperceives an utterance, the misperception is not directly available for inspection. Rather, what is available is a listener's report of a misperception. This report may be subject to modification or interpretation, whether unconscious or conscious. It is a report of a misperception rather than a misperception.

It would seem that we know neither what the speaker said nor what the listener heard. Instead, we have access only to intentions and reports. Yet such difficulties and ambiguities are not peculiar to speech errors. Any data based on anecdotal report and uncontrolled observation suffer from the same limitations.

Slips of the ear are worth examining because they provide a unique window into the ordinary use of language in everyday circumstances. Needless to say, any one example of an error should be treated with caution.

1.4. OTHER STUDIES OF MISPERCEPTIONS

Collections and descriptions of misperceptions in ordinary conversation are less common than collections of errors in speech production. These reports typically examine perceptual errors from one point of view or collect errors in response to specific hypotheses.

The first collections of errors in speech were compiled by Meringer (1908) and by Meringer and Mayer (1895). These collections were in German, primarily devoted to slips of the tongue. They also included 47 slips of the ear, or *Verhören*.

The perceptual errors were translated and analyzed by Celce-Murcia (1980). In her report, Celce-Murcia also included a number of errors which she had observed. Although the Meringer and Mayer corpus of misperceptions is small, one generalization which it suggested has been corroborated repeatedly. Meringer (1908) observed that the vowels of root syllables and vowels in general tend to be perceived correctly whereas consonants are misperceived more readily.

Although Meringer and Mayer do not discuss examples of misperceptions beyond this generalization, Celce-Murcia (1980) points out that their corpus includes errors in which the target utterance is quite different from the perceived utterance. For example, Meringer (1908) heard "Durst oder Hunger" (thirst or hunger) for "Verdruss oder Kummer" (dismay or sorrow) [quoted and translated by Celce-Murcia, 1980]. Many of the errors involve proper names, and many show grammatical coherence coupled with a lack of appropriateness to the situation or conversation.

In discussing the Meringer and Mayer corpus and her own examples of slips of the ear, Celce-Murcia (1980) offered some suggestions about the causes of misperceptions. One possibility is that the speaker and the listener use a different dialect of their language. Listener expectations and background knowledge may also play a causative role in misperceptions.

Browman (1980) analyzed a corpus of approximately 200 misperceptions. She was interested in the most general description to which the data were amenable, focusing on the position of errors within words, disregarding possible differences between errors which affect one word or more than one word. Under this analysis, Browman concluded that vowels and consonants were equally likely to be misperceived and that misperceptions were equally distributed across all positions within words.

Browman also distinguished between errors caused by acoustic (or phonetic) misanalysis and by lexical decision, finding that errors which are lexically based tend to preserve accurately the initial and final segments of words. Her observations are based on the assumption that words are natural perceptual units processed from beginning to end, and thus her observations do not extend to slips which cross word boundaries or involve changes in the order of segments. Browman suggests that these properties of misperceptions require further investigation.

Labov and his colleagues have collected almost 700 slips of the ear, which Labov (1994) terms natural misunderstandings; his focus is not on the relationship between linguistic structure and psychological processes but rather on misperceptions as a data for understanding language change.

In particular, Labov is concerned with misperceptions related to dialect differences. In his data set, Labov (1994) found that approximately 27% of the errors are traceable to dialect differences, though this proportion is probably inflated because of the interests of the reporters (p. 273). Labov classified the misperceptions as global misunderstandings and local misunderstandings: "When the phonetic conditions are truly degenerate, the report shows massive misunderstandings where only a few stressed syllables of the original utterance are preserved" (p. 274). For example,

> The mayor found an answer for the Eagles →
> Ralph Nader found an answer for the needles (p. 274).

A local misunderstanding depends on the misinterpretation of a specific segment. According to Labov, this is most likely due to the phonetic realization of that segment. For example,

The house has a yellow door and lattice windows → lettuce windows (p. 274).

Labov suggests that many of the slips can be explained by reference to four consonantal environments which are known to affect the realizations of vowels. These environments are following nasal consonants, following /l/, following /r/, and preceding obstruent plus liquid clusters. These environments tend to reduce the phonetic distance between vowels and so promote misunderstandings.

Although Labov's focus is on dialect differences and language change, the slips given in his data set are similar to those appearing in other collections.

Voss (1984) has approached the study of slips of the ear experimentally, investigating the perception of English by native speakers of German who are also proficient in English.

In his first experiment, Voss examined the perceptual effects of hesitations. Voss asked listeners to transcribe in English orthography an excerpt from a television interview. As is characteristic of natural speech, the passage contained various kinds of hesitations: repeats, false starts, filled pauses, and unfilled pauses. Almost a third of the slips originated in a misinterpretation of hesitation (p. 58). In some cases, hesitations were mistaken for words or parts of words. For example, the target *for—say activities* was reported as *for their activities* and *for fair activities*. In this example, listeners interpreted the hesitation word *say* as part of the discourse (p. 59). The reverse error was also observed.

The target *such as—boat building* was repeated as *such as building,* treating the word *boat* as a partial repetition of *building*. This is an intriguing finding. Unfortunately, it is almost impossible to know how often hesitations are responsible for slips of the ear in casual conversation.

Voss' second experiment (1984) examined the effect of regional speech characteristics on nonnative listeners. The recording employed was from a children's radio program, which "is characterized by narrative interspersed with dialogue; the whole text is performed by the same speaker, who, however, sets the dialogues or direct speech insets off from the narrative by assigning different regional speech stereotypes to the various characters of the story" (p. 66). As is true of English dialects in general, the differences were primarily associated with vowels. When Voss examined the slips supplied by his listeners, he found that deviations from "standard" pronunciation coincided with clusters of errors (p. 71). Misperceptions of vowel segments tended to involve those vowels which are responsible for the regional speech effects (p. 74). For example, the target *people* [ɛ] *to think* was reported as *paper to think* and *pay but to think,* among other misperceptions.

Voss' third experiment (1984) compared the types of errors listeners reported to their native language, German, with errors they reported to English. All types of slips which were observed in the nonnative error corpus were also found in the native corpus, implying that the same listener strategies were found in both speech perception situations (p. 113). The slips which the listeners reported for both languages were similar in type to slips reported in other collections with one exception. Not reported previously were paraphrases, misperceptions involving potentially multiple segments but approximately equivalent meaning. For example,

one of the problems—erm—of people → one of the problems for people.

Voss' experiments provide valuable data on several levels. Not least, it is worth noting that Voss' listeners reported the same kinds of errors under controlled response and material conditions as listeners have reported in the perception of casual, evanescent conversation. This finding increases our confidence in the data provided by slips of the ear.

1.5. PLAN OF THE BOOK

The data are presented separately for adults and for children according to error type. First, the focus is on the segment; simple vowel and consonant errors are described as well as segmental errors which are part of complex misperceptions. Then the focus is placed on errors in the perception of the shapes of words, detailing many of the properties of complex misperceptions. The interaction of misperceptions with syntactic, morphological, and lexical knowledge is discussed. Perceptual errors made by children are described separately. Finally, some implications of the data for theories of speech perception and language understanding are considered.

Experimental data validating some properties of slips of the ear are described in Appendix A. All examples of slips of the ear are listed in Appendix B.

CHAPTER 2

Vowel Misperceptions

Vowels in general are most frequently perceived correctly.
—Meringer and Mayer (1895)

Vowels were rarely misperceived unless other errors were present as well. That is, there were few examples of pure vowel errors. More commonly, vowel errors occurred as part of more complex misperceptions involving consonants, other vowels, or the overall structure of the target word.

2.1. PURE VOWEL ERRORS

Adult vowel misperceptions comprised a minuscule 5% of the total corpus of errors. The majority of vowel errors occurred in stressed syllables. Only six errors involved an unstressed vowel exclusively.

2.1.1. ERRORS IN UNSTRESSED SYLLABLES

The examples of unstressed vowel errors are listed in Table 2.1. Approximately half of the errors affected unstressed function words, and the other half occurred in unstressed syllables of polysyllabic words. These were the only errors in the corpus affecting vowels or unstressed syllables exclusively.

TABLE 2.1   Misperceptions of Unstressed Syllables

He's going to write a paper on tonology → on tenology

grammar workshop → grandma workshop

her system collapsed → her sister collapsed

Verner → Verna

Beowulf is received by Hrothgar in Heorot → by Hrothgar and Heorot

He's an ENT → an E and T

swimming and Greek → swimming in Greek

2.1.2. ERRORS IN STRESSED SYLLABLES

The place of articulation of the stressed syllable nuclei which served as targets for misperceptions was distributed unequally between front vowels and other vowels. Central and back vowels were misperceived approximately equally, but much less frequently than front vowels. Errors involving phonemic diphthongs were the least common. All of the front vowels appeared with approximately equal frequency as sources of error. However, only the two back vowels /a/ and /o/ were misperceived. These proportions are different from what would be expected on strictly distributional grounds, in that Shriberg and Kent (1982) report that only about 14% of vowels in conversational speech are front vowels. However, since the total number of vowel errors was small, it is quite possible that the skewed distribution represents sampling error.

2.1.2.1. Errors in Vowel Height

Of all vowel misperceptions, errors affecting vowel height were the most common. Table 2.2 lists all examples of adult errors in the perception of vowel height. Apparently, errors in both directions occurred with equal frequency.

Some of the errors undoubtedly resulted from simple effects of phonetic context. Many of the vowel height misperceptions occurred in syllables with a tautosyllabic nasal, a phonetic environment which obscures the formant structure of vowels. The same effect may be attributed to /r/ and /l/ (see Bond, 1976a, 1976b; Labov, 1994).

Some of the errors probably resulted from dialect differences. The phonetic effects of the nasal consonants may have been augmented by dialect differences concerning possible vowel contrasts before nasals. For example, /ɪ/ and /ɛ/ and to a lesser extent /æ/ tend to merge before nasal consonants in some varieties of American English. Errors such as

kings → kangs

TABLE 2.2   Vowel Height Errors

<u>Lower vowel to higher vowel</u>

where we went to the horse show → horse shoe

Flashman's → Fleshman's

You're very fickle → very fecal

The bell isn't working → the bill

There are some cattle farmers → kettle farmers

That's a special → spatial

Cherri and me → Cheery and me

Swaney → Sweeney

Jan → Gene

Wendy will come → Windy

swimming and Greek → swimming in Greek

Alan → Ellen

some are better → bitter

The British have light l's → ales

Are you a barn member? → born member

<u>Higher vowel to lower vowel</u>

a lot of nude beaches → nude bitches

I don't know if we have any more "trecks" left → tracks left

Vowels are a whole 'nother kettle of fish → cattle of fish

sheik-like → shake-like

kings → kangs

Gene → Jan

Beowulf is received by Hrothgar in Heorot → by Hrothgar and Heorot

He's an ENT → an E and T

may therefore have resulted from indistinct vowel formants as well as from uncertainty about the dialect characteristics of the speaker.

In southeastern Ohio, most front lax vowels become tense before the consonants /ʃ/ and /tʃ/, among others. It is possible therefore that in the error

That's a special → spatial

the listener failed to compensate for a dialect feature of the speaker, not realizing that the speaker was employing tense vowels in this particular environment.

2.1.2.2. Errors in the Tense–Lax Dimension

Errors affecting the tense–lax dimension were relatively rare in the adult data. The tokens are listed in Table 2.3. These have also been listed as vowel height errors since the traditional vowel quadrilateral implies that tense vowels are higher than corresponding lax vowels. If tenseness errors are taken at face value, then it is just as likely for a tense vowel to be perceived as a lax vowel as it is for the reverse error to occur.

2.1.2.3. Errors in the Front–Back Dimension

Although front vowels served as targets for misperceptions more often than either central or back vowels, front vowel errors almost always involved either vowel height or tenseness. Front vowels were rarely misperceived as back or central vowels, but there were three tokens of front vowels being misidentified as diphthongs.

Of the three stressed back vowel misperceptions involving the front–back dimension, one back vowel target was misperceived as a front vowel and two as diphthongs. The stressed central vowel /ʌ/ also occurred as a target in a few front–back errors. Of the two errors with central vowel targets, one was misperceived as a front vowel and the second as a back vowel. These errors are given in Table 2.4.

One of the back vowel errors was probably a result of dialect confusion:

Wattsvile → Whitesville.

The listener from Ohio, only somewhat familiar with the speech of someone from North Carolina, may be attempting to compensate for a monophthongized /ai/. The Ohioan did not realize that no compensation is necessary for this place name.

TABLE 2.3   Tenseness Errors

Tense to lax

a lot of nude beaches → nude bitches

We'll get a house → will get a house

Lax to tense

You're very fickle → very fecal

That's a special → spatial

The British have light l's → ales

TABLE 2.4 Errors in the Front–Back Dimension

It really turned wet out → white out

It's a chain tool → chine tool

It's like a math problem → mouth problem

Wattsville → Whitesville [North Carolina to Ohio]

This blond guy in my class → blind guy

Pete Johnson → Jensen

Did I ever tell you about this usher? → this esher

color → collar

I went nuts → I want nuts

There were three errors that involve vowels commonly described as rhotacized. In two of these errors, an unstressed rhotacized vowel was perceived as /ə/:

Grammar Workshop → grandma workshop

Verner → Verna.

In the other two cases, a stressed, rhotacized vowel /ɝ/ was perceived as a back vowel followed by /r/:

Stir this → store this

Favorite kind of shirts → kind of shorts.

Exactly how these errors are to be described is considerably influenced by the assumptions one makes about the nature of the syllable nucleus in the words *stir* and *shirt*.

Only a few diphthong targets were misperceived:

What's wrong with her bike? → her back

You know that soil can be . . . → swail can be

I wanna catch Lloyd Rice → Lord Rice.

2.2. VOWEL ERRORS AS PART OF COMPLEX ERRORS

In vowel misperceptions which occurred in connection with other misperceptions, the number of errors increased and the phonetic transparency of the error decreased.

2.2.1. Unstressed Vowel Errors

There were a great many examples of unstressed vowel errors accompanied by other errors, either consonantal or in word boundary assignment. Of these, most occurred in content words under circumstances in which it was relatively clear which syllable of the target utterance was involved in the error. In the remaining errors, the match between the target and the misperception was more remote.

Some of the function word errors may be cases of "editing," that is, the listener reporting a function word which is appropriate to the context as otherwise identified. In the example

attacks in the ear → a tax on the ear,

the appropriate function word *on* rather than *in* is reported following *tax*. However, not all function word misperceptions were a simple result of eliminating a syntactic problem which occurred because of another misperception. The example

from 180 some → for 180 some

indicates that the phonetic composition of a preposition may be misperceived in and of itself. This type of error is not very common however.

The misperceptions of unstressed syllables in content words which can be clearly matched with the targets often involved errors in the perception of consonants as well. A large proportion of the targets were probably produced with a short, indistinct vowel or as syllabic consonants. It is difficult to find any general pattern for the errors. Apart from being unstressed vowels, the targets did not have any clear characteristics in common. The misperceptions often involved so many other changes that the nature of the unstressed vowel seems to be almost irrelevant. These data are given in Table 2.5.

2.2.2. Stressed Vowel Errors

In the stressed vowel errors, front vowels were targets more often than back vowels. Central vowels and diphthongs were targets least often. In addition, there were three examples of a stressed vowel being perceived without any corresponding vowel being present in the target utterance.

Of the front vowel errors, only a few affected function words; the remainder affected content words. By far the most common targets were the lax vowels. The two vowels /ɪ/ and /ɛ/ were error targets approximately equally often, while the vowel /æ/ was a target less frequently.

TABLE 2.5   Unstressed Vowel Errors in Combination with Other Errors

In function word

Couldn't you say that was an SPC? → was misperceived?

from 180 some → for 180 some

the radio on → the regular one

we eat at eight → we needed eight

it costs six to seven dollars to replace → sixty-seven dollars

We are not using the accident rates yet → not using the accident rate shit

this Acoustical Society → the sacoustical society

I know where the place is → what the place is

four to five weeks → forty-five weeks

attacks in the ear → a tax on the ear

the OED → DOED

with drugs → at stud

this nation → the station

Sonic, the hedgehog → son of the hedgehog

He was in a wreck → Iraq

In content word, misperceived syllable can be identified

Who's calling? → Who's Colleen?

name is being withheld → repelled

Wardhaugh → Wardhol

cathedral → gazebo

her system collapsed → her sister collapsed

Southern California → summit California

Jakarta → Chicago [British speaker]

bubonic → Blue Bonnet

an imitative → an inervative

glottal wave of the deaf → auto wave of the deaf

Latvian festival → Latvian Eskimo

Nelson → Neusa

Dr. Dierker → Dr. Diargood

look at the cloud cover → card cover

a diet to increase my sexual potency → to appease my sexual potency

honors political science course → honest political science course

savor → sable

interestin' → Enarson

interview → ennerview

(*Continues*)

TABLE 2.5   (*Continued*)

my appointment was rather long → running long

the habitat → the havercamp

How about your tires? → your title

a U-Haul in front of us → an ink ball in front of us

Chris Evert at Wimbledon → Prince Edward

I kept an eye on the Big Dipper last night → I kept denying the Big Dipper

Get a pill out → a pillow

Mad River Township → Madrigal Township

I just like it → I dislike it

I'm horny → it's morning

eat a Maple Leaf wiener → a make-believe wiener

Olga's son → the sun

See the giant meadow muffin → metal muffin

The book I would recommend is by Paul Zemmlin → Zemler

the anechoic chamber → the ambionic chamber

four wheat pennies → four weekends

living with a coach → women who coach

they took footprints when you're born → they took footprints in the dorm

I need to talk to him → I need to calculate

a linguini is a noodle → a lean Wheatie is a noodle

the Clemency Information Center → the Columbus Information Center

meteor → meat eater

<u>Syllables difficult to match</u>

That's an *L* → an *A–O*

orgasm → organism

We're going to stay in Tebins → in tenements

imagery → energy

A lot of kids are going to Oswego → to Sweden

I love you and my baby → I love you. You are my baby

Herbert H. Lehman College → Heritage Lehman College

Geez, really? → Disraeli

That's a good way to get your car door taken off → your carburetor taken off

low visibility → lovas

portrait → poetry [speaker is British]

John Eulenberg → John Gilbert

just bisecting lines → just bicycling

The misperception patterns did not appear to be different for those for isolated vowel errors. Vowel height errors were the most common by far, whereas errors in the front–back dimension were rare. Many of the errors occurred in words containing consonants which tend to obscure vowel identity such as /r/, /l/, and the nasals. All errors for front vowel targets are given in Table 2.6.

Back vowel targets were more evenly distributed between the tense and the lax vowels. Most lax vowel errors affected the targets /a/ and /ɔ/, the latter always followed by /r/, a vowel which is phonetically quite variable (Bond, 1976b). This vowel was always perceived as a higher vowel. The most common error for the target /a/ was /æ/. Half of the misperceptions of target /u/ were front vowels. Many of the misperceived vowels were associated with /l/ or a nasal consonant. These patterns suggest a phonetic basis for at least some of the misperceptions. The data are given in Table 2.7.

There is one curious misperception in these data:

$$\text{barbell set} \rightarrow \text{bord la sell.}$$

After noting the misperception, the listener commented that he thought the speaker had said something in a different language. This error is the one of the very few in which a listener mistakes the language of the utterance but develops a phonological representation for it nevertheless.

There were only nine errors for the central vowels. The syllables in which the misperceived /ɝ/ occurred were either followed by a nasal or by /l/, suggesting a phonetic basis for the misperceptions. The errors for target /ʌ/ were much more varied. These data are given in Table 2.8.

Of the misperceptions of diphthong targets, there was only one error for the diphthong /oi/. The remaining errors were almost equally divided between /ai/ and /au/. The vowel /ɛ/ was most commonly substituted for the /ai/, and the vowel /a/ for /au/. These patterns suggest that at least some of the errors were brought about by dialect variation. Many speakers of American English monophthongize the two diphthongs, producing a low front vowel instead. This vowel was apparently identified as the most appropriate monophthong by the listeners. The data are given in Table 2.9.

2.2.3. STRESSED and UNSTRESSED VOWELS

Table 2.10 lists all 13 examples of misperceptions in which both stressed and unstressed vowels were affected. The errors seem to be quite similar to errors which affect only one vowel. Though the mismatch between the target and the misperception was obviously greater, the errors did not seem to involve any new principles.

TABLE 2.6   Errors for Front Vowel Targets

In function words

Did you put the food out for him? → for them

no she isn't → no shitting

In four to six months we'll get a house → four to six marks will get you a house

When were you here? → Why were you here?

there up ahead → clear up ahead

I get to leave this place → I can't believe this place

That's a good idea for the future → What's a good idea

Vowel target /ɪ/

illegible → illogical

Givon → pavanne

Texas Women's University → Texas Lumens University

conditions are almost right → Hendersons are almost right

Debbie is fifth → is first

Finn → friend

the Old Creek Inn was deserted → creek end was deserted

kings → cans

a big heavy ring → a big heavy rain

It's going to ring in a minute → rain in a minute

my coffee cup refilled → my coffee cup fell

missed the news → must a snoozed

I have a weed trimmer → I have a weak tremor

Vowel target /ɛ/

mental science → middle science

I tripped on a tent pole → tadpole

toast and jelly → toast and chili

too close to melt → to mouth

boiled these pearls in cherry preserves → in chili preserves

How does the west look? → the bus look

inflection → inflation

an exam at Kent State → Wayne State

I'm not American → not a miracle

Mrs. Herrell → Mrs. Hill

I think it's a penguin → a pink one

(Continues)

TABLE 2.6   (*Continued*)

It will be done next year → in six years

Bette Midler → Pat Miller

I didn't have to wear a coat → to work

barrel → bottle

I need air → I need ear muffs

your etiquette books → your other cook books

Dec man tomorrow → Pacman tomorrow

Vowel target /æ/

your ladder → your letter

wrapping service → wrecking service

shabby furniture → Chevy furniture

Levi Jackson → Levi Jetson

a slant board → a sled board

meet Mr. Anderson → Mr. Edison

think about your valves → vowels

Those are nice pants → nice peanuts

We got our task force grant → our tennis court grant

Wrangler → regular

Avalanche → evelinsh

Tense vowel targets

I have to eat too → I have eighty-two

I feel secure → I disappear

Anyone who thinks carob bean is a good substitute for chocolate is crazy → paraffin is a good substitute

I'm serious → I'm furious

I'm staying near O'Hare → more O'Hare

her fiance's Canadian → comedian

I say crayon → crown

I already claimed it → cleaned it

TABLE 2.7   Errors for Back Vowel Targets

Vowel target /ʊ/

pull course → cool course

Vowel target /ɔ/

passed with a four → with a full

one of the court poets → the poor poets

What's another word for menorah → for manure

It's always too short → always toujours

How's your work going? → book going

worse 'n that → where's Annette

Vowel target /a/

about some follow-up → some foul-up

Bruce Galtter → Bruce Bladder

barbell set → bord la sell

off → up

It's that lousy atomic bread I can't stand → Italian bread

"osill" → ass hole

Falstaff → Flagstaff

we offered six → we Alfred six

You swallowed a watermelon → You smiled at a watermelon

bookshop → bookshelf

a small computer → a smoke computer

Vowel target /u/

I have to go to the moon at six → to the mint at six

a loose end in this problem → a leaf's end

everybody's human → everybody's showman

Trudy → tree

boustrophedonic → Posturepedic

I was through on a bus → I was thrown off a bus

on neurolinguistics → on zero linguistics

we had a representative of the preschool come → of the Peace Corps

Vowel target /o/

the PON → the PLN

sewing it → selling it

(Continues)

TABLE 2.7 (*Continued*)

I wouldn't eat at the restaurant in a motel unless it's snowing → unless it's smelly

loan word → long word

Dover sole → Dover salad

Ann was afraid to go → afraid to do it

Is that home baked? → Is that hard to bake?

TABLE 2.8 Errors for Central Vowel Targets

rural free delivery → oral free delivery

The urn is finished → the urine is finished

German's looking for a room → Jim's looking

get my other cookbooks → my etiquette books

Pier One Imports → beer wine imports

foxglove → fox globe

foxglove → fox glow

they're all nuts → all nice

hockey pucks → coffee pots

The errors which involved perceptually adding a stressed syllable to the target utterance were the following:

five-sixths of all conversions in the church → of all conversations

psychic → psychotic

Riga → eureka

I need air → I need earmuffs.

If the listener misperceived *air* as *ear,* then adding the content syllable *muffs* involved an attempt to arrive at a plausible lexical item, perhaps by association.

2.2.4. RHOTACIZED VOWELS

There were examples of a vowel plus /r/ sequence being perceived as a schwar. All of the targets occurred in stressed syllables; four were perceived as stressed syllables, two as unstressed. There was one example of an /r/ apparently shifting from the beginning to the end of a syllable:

Astrid Gilberto → bastard Gilberto.

These data are given in Table 2.11.

TABLE 2.9   Errors for Diphthong Targets

<table>
<tr><td colspan="1" align="center">Diphthong target /ai/</td></tr>
</table>

Hyman → Lehmann

lighter → ladder

she's ripe → she's raped

Try newspaper and a hot iron → hot air

plant dying → plant dung

They're all Appalachian whites → Appalachian waste

Dec writer → decorator

Star Fire → /sta fa/

<table>
<tr><td align="center">Diphthong target /au/</td></tr>
</table>

I found it → Icelandic

cloudy → ploddy

two hundred hours → two hundred dollars

Let me now try to develop this point → not try to develop

I'm on a trip now → a chip one

still lousy → still assy

Do you have any Wite-Out? → white album

<table>
<tr><td align="center">Diphthong target /ɔi/</td></tr>
</table>

Hello, big boy → big Bart

2.2.5. SYLLABIC /l/

Although traditionally, /l/ is treated as a consonant, word-final /l/ in English is almost always syllabic and often vocalized, that is, produced as a high back vowel. In the vowel misperception data, there were a few examples of syllabic /l/ interacting with back vowels:

> Sunoco has a battery → snorkel has a battery
> Wardhaugh → Wardhol
> That's an *L* → an *A–O*
> mail → mayo
> Old Navy store → oak baby store.

In the first examples, a back vowel is perceived as /l/. The second two examples exhibit the reverse error, leading to the perception of an additional syllable. In the final example, the /l/ appears to be absorbed by the vowel.

TABLE 2.10   Stressed and Unstressed Vowel Errors

---

setting up of time → studying of time

hero sandwich → harrah sandwich

SUNOCO has a battery → snorkel has a battery

AFIT /æfɪt/ → effort

the pony league → pointer league

I have a dental appointment → a dinner appointment

the Codofil people → the colorful people

Is that margarine? → Is that Mondrian?

Wouldn't she look good with a ring in her nose → oregano nose

I'll catch my breath here → catch my breakfast

I'll catch my breath here → my brush up

the paramour → the power mower

kills germs where they grow → kills germs with egg roll

TABLE 2.11   Fusion of Vowel and /r/

---

go to a party → to a burly

trying to get over being chairman → being German

the Arabs and the Israelis → herbs and the Israelis

He could run his son → burn his son

Astrid Gilberto → bastard Gilberto

They had a ten-year party → a tenure party

He got ten years in prison → tenure in prison

It is possible that the misperception

Nelson → Neusa

is also related to vocalized /l/, in this case in syllable-final position.

2.3. GENERAL PROPERTIES OF VOWEL
ERRORS

Mostof the misperceptions affected stressed vowels. Though the number of tokens on which generalizations can be based was quite small, vowel height errors were the most common.

A portion of the vowel errors probably resulted from indistinct phonetic information as a consequence of specific consonantal environments, particularly the nasals and liquids, which obscured to some degree the formant structure of vowels. Another portion of the misperceptions probably resulted from dialect differences between speakers and listeners. These errors suggest that listeners use knowledge of dialect variation to interpret the phonetic characteristics of vowels. The most interesting observation concerning vowel errors is that they were relatively rare in the total corpus. Since vowels are often longer and more intense than surrounding consonants, their resilience to misperceptions should perhaps not be surprising. The misperception data agree with experimental findings and theoretical arguments for the suggestion that stressed vowels provide reliable information for word identity.

Bond (1981) found that deliberate mispronunciations of stressed vowels in short paragraphs led to more disruption of comprehension than did various kinds of mispronunciations of consonants. Bond and Small (1983) asked subjects to shadow passages which contained mispronounced consonants and stressed vowels. Subjects had little difficulty recovering the intended words when they contained mispronounced consonants but recovered only 15% of the words containing mispronounced vowels. These data suggest that vowel mispronunciations are disruptive, hence that stressed vowels provide reliable phonetic information.

Pisoni (1981) argued that stressed syllables provide an "island of reliability," that is, reliable phonetic information, which listeners use to interpret the stream of speech. In a similar vein, Grosjean and Gee (1987) and Cutler and Norris (1988) suggest that stressed syllables are used to initiate a lexical search.

The scarcity of vowel misperceptions certainly support these suggestions. Listeners seem to pay attention to stressed vowels as sources of reliable information for finding words in the stream of speech.

CHAPTER 3

Consonant Misperceptions

It is striking what small effects the consonants . . . have . . .
—Meringer and Mayer (1895)

Consonant errors occurred in considerably greater numbers than vowel errors. Consequently, generalizations which can be made on the basis of the data are much more robust.

3.1. SIMPLE CONSONANT ERRORS

The consonant errors can be classified according to three perceptual categories: deletions, additions, and substitutions. In a deletion error, a listener does not hear anything corresponding to a consonant present in the target word. In an addition error, the listener reports hearing a spurious consonant, a consonant which has no analogue in the target word. In a substitution, a perceived consonant does not match the target in place, manner, or voicing.

In terms of position of occurrence, the majority of simple consonant errors were word-initial ones. There were somewhat fewer word-final errors, while medial errors were the least common. More than half of the errors affected plosives. Target fricatives were the next most common. The remaining manners of articulation served as targets for misperceptions much less frequently. Labial and alveolar consonants were the most common place of articulation for mis-perceived consonants. The manner of articulation of misperceived target consonants was not related to their frequency of occurrence in English. Though stops and fricatives are the most common manners of articulation found in conversational English (Shriberg & Kent, 1982), their occurrence in perceptual errors was greater than their occurrence in conversational English would suggest. The place of articulation of targets for errors also did not correspond strictly with expectation from conversational English.

3.1.1. Perceptual Loss of Consonants

Half of the deleted target consonants were voiceless, and half were voiced. Further, approximately half of the deletions affected singletons, while half affected consonants which were members of clusters. Deletion errors were not equally likely to occur in all word positions; rather, deletions in final position were the most common. This distribution opposes the general tendency for more initial errors. Perhaps the reasons are essentially phonetic. Consonants in final position may optionally be produced rather indistinctly; for example, stops may be unreleased and voiced fricatives partially devoiced. It is possible that these relatively weakly articulated consonants were simply not heard by listeners even though vowels tend to provide reliable information about following consonants.

All tokens of deletion errors are given in Table 3.1.

For some of the word-initial errors, there was no characteristic of the phonetic environment which would tend to promote the perceptual loss of the consonant. For example,

They're all power people → our people

is an error in which the loss of the initial stop apparently was not caused by any phonetic property of the target utterance. For other deletion errors, phonetic explanations can be suggested. Two errors involved almost identical deletions of a consonant in a cluster:

What are those sticks? → those ticks
and so has Stinziano → Tinziano.

These may have resulted from mistaken word boundary assignment. In each case, the listener may have assigned the fricative to one word rather than distributing it between two.

It is likely that the two medial errors

We're talking about the winter of '75 → winner of '75
Andy's going to fall asleep → Annie's going to

both resulted from characteristics of American English phonology. In casual conversational speech, nasal plus obstruent clusters are commonly reduced to

TABLE 3.1   Consonant Loss

Word-initial

who? → /u/

When their condition → air condition

Wie geht's → i gates

They're all power people → our people

We're going to go around and frenetically pick up the living room → phonetically pick up the
   living room

I'm a phrenologist → phonologist

What are those sticks? → those ticks

some rice → some ice

and so has Stinziano → Tinziano

Word-medial

striking San Francisco doctors → dockers

We're talking about the winter of '75 → winner of '75

Andy's going to fall asleep → Annie's going to fall asleep

Wilmington → Willington

studying Javanese internally → studying Javanese eternally

insufficient → inefficient

Word-final

two twenty-eight → two twenty a

Noam Chomsky leads a double life → double lie

move → moo

I saw a rusty old cart → car

Did you hear the guide in the Bishop White House? → the guy in the Bishop White House

It's going to be offered by Eastern → Easter

train → tray

in harmony with the text → test

the nodes of the moon → the nose

Do you know what geodes are? → G O's

Mr. Sands mother's neighbor → Mr. Sans

She writes comments on our papers → comets

houseplants → house plans

plain talk → play talk

---

a nasal, deleting the obstruent. The two errors can be attributed to the listeners' failure to compensate for the cluster reduction present in the target utterance.

Three of the word-final consonant deletions involved nasal plus obstruent clusters as targets, in which the speaker presumably had reduced the cluster but the listener had not compensated for the reduction. Given this explanation, however, the token

> She writes comments on our papers → she writes comets

is anomalous in that the listener reported hearing the obstruent, not the nasal. However, *comets* is an English lexical item, while *comens* is not.

Three other deletion errors may also be a result of English phonological processes. It is common for speakers to reduce final obstruent clusters so that words such as *text* may be pronounced /tɛst/. Then the listener's error in the example

> in harmony with the text → test,

as well as in other tokens involving final consonant clusters, may have consisted of not compensating for the reductions made by the speaker.

3.1.2. Perceptual Addition of Consonants

The addition of consonants is the inverse of deletion: a listener reports a consonant which was not present in the target utterance. Additions were approximately as common as deletions. Spurious consonants were rarely perceived in consonant clusters, though it was possible for additions to create clusters. There were almost twice as many voiced consonants added as voiceless ones. The addition errors occurred initially, medially, and finally in about equal proportions. All tokens of perceptual addition of consonants are given in Table 3.2.

All of the voiceless consonant additions in word-initial position are in environments which suggest no phonetic reasons for the additions. Three of the voiced consonant additions may result from erroneous word boundary assignments:

> Slip of the ear → slip of the year
> The article → the yarticle
> Finger in your ear → in your rear.

In each case, it is possible that the listener interpreted the final segment of the word preceding the target as also a word-initial glide, distributing a single consonant over two words.

In two of the medial errors, the listener interpreted a nasal to be a reduced nasal plus obstruent cluster, as in the misperception

> Mrs. Winner → Winter.

TABLE 3.2   Consonant Addition

Word-initial

The only thing it doesn't work with for us is onions → bunions

Write the word "osill" → fossil

slip of the ear → slip of the year

the article → the yarticle

You leave too much air in there → hair

has been cool and collected → cruel and collected

too much air → too much hair

finger in your ear → in your rear

Do you have ice? → rice

Word-medial

It's Lawson → Larson

Kamasutra → *Karmasutra*

Mr. Hawbecker → Mr. Holbecker

I just talked to her and saw Maria → Marina

A basket of apples → amples

sitter problems → sinter

Mrs. Winner → Winter

fine sunny weather → fine Sunday weather

Word-final

How many moos did A. get? → moves did A. get?

This picture does justice to Pei → Peg

the white sauce ladies → the white socks ladies

back to the grass roots → the grasp roots

My name is Goes, like walk → Ghost

You can weld with it—braze → braids

They can take cars to school → cards

What kind of pans did you use →pants

They drop their G's → their jeans

I can see you at four → I can't see you at four

Rudal → Rudolf

These errors appear to be the perceptual inverse of deletion errors in the nasal plus obstruent environment. The listener employed knowledge of English phonology to compensate for a presumably reduced stretch of speech. In these cases, however, phonological knowledge is used in inappropriate circumstances.

The error

It's Lawson → Larson

probably stems from dialect differences. The speaker is from the east coast of the United States and from a region where people are known to employ an r-less dialect of American English. The listener's error arose from attempting to compensate for this dialect feature, but in this case the compensation was inappropriate. The remaining addition errors are difficult to explain. For example, a spurious nasal was heard in the error

sitter problems → sinter

as well as in two similar tokens. In two other examples, spurious liquids were added. Neither phonological nor phonetic explanations for such errors are readily available.

As in the case of medial errors, several of the final consonant additions may result from compensating for a supposed consonant cluster reduction. Two errors seem to have resulted from compensating for reduced nasal plus obstruent clusters:

What kind of pans did you use? → pants
I can see you at four → I can't see you at four.

Five errors probably resulted from the listener's assumption that a word final obstruent represents a reduced cluster, as in the example

You can weld with it—braze → braids.

The listener may have considered the final fricative of *braze* to represent a reduced obstruent cluster.

3.1.3. MANNER OF ARTICULATION SUBSTITUTIONS

Perceptual errors in the manner of articulation of consonants were relatively common. More than one-third of the errors involved mistaking the manner of articulation of a target consonant, though the manner error was sometimes accompanied by a voicing and place error as well. Stops and fricatives were affected most often. Errors were almost twice as common in initial position as medially or in final position. Phonetic or phonological explanations for most manner errors were not obvious; the target and substitute consonants did, however, tend to resemble each other phonetically.

3.1.3.1. Manner Errors for Obstruents

In general, obstruents tended to be perceived as obstruents, and the most common manner errors by far were misperceptions of target stops as fricatives. Manner errors for stop targets are given in Table 3.3. In word-initial position, besides

TABLE 3.3   Manner Substitutions for Plosives

Initial stops perceived as fricatives

chicken poulette → chicken filet

She'll be home in about half an hour if I know her pace → her face

He's got a CB too → CV too

Tagalog → Thagalog

a poor house → a whore house

Captain Cook → Captain Hook

ballistic conditions → felistic conditions

Duke of Buckingham → Duke of Fuckingham

Bay Village → Faye Village

She had on a trench suit → a French suit

DC-9 → VC-9

Gary Dalton → very Dalton

All of the members grew up in Philadelphia → threw up

Curt → hurt

Dr. Garber → Dr. Harber

Initial stops perceived as affricates

I'll bet that'll be a teary program → cheery program

Garnes → /dʒarnes/

Word-medial plosives

There's a car named the Roadrunner → the Roserunner

booty → boolie

sitting here for the last two hours snipping dates → sniffing dates

Word-final stops perceived as fricatives

Bloomfield's personality was warped here → Whorfed here

I want to go out to Wilderness Trace and buy a cup → buy a cuff

It looks like it's carved of teak → teeth

He must be a good Greek → good grief

We start our summer league tonight → summer leave

Word-final stops perceived as nasals

Have you seen Rod lately? → Ron lately

Fifth Street → fifth string

If it wasn't a humid country → human country

the most common stop fricative misperceptions, stop targets were perceived as affricates. Of all these errors, nearly half involved not only a manner but a voicing error as well. In manner errors, labial stops were the most frequent targets. Alveolar and velar stops were error targets less frequently.

In the medial misperception, a voiceless alveolar stop /t/ was perceived as a lateral:

$$booty \rightarrow boolie.$$

The target stop was probably produced as an alveolar flap.

In final position, stops were perceived as fricatives and as nasals. In the errors leading to fricatives, the targets were the stops /p,k,g/. Voicing was perceived correctly in each case. When stops were perceived as nasals, two of the targets were /d/, perceived as /n/.

Affricates were involved as targets in only a few manner errors—one in initial position, two medially, and one finally. Initially, a voiced affricate was perceived as a voiceless stop:

$$I \text{ wonder where Jimmy is going?} \rightarrow \text{Timmy is going.}$$

In medial and final position, the errors resulted in perceived fricatives, maintaining voicing:

$$dialect\ divergence \rightarrow dialect\ diversions$$
$$You\ are\ hearing\ Appalachian \rightarrow appellation$$
$$\textit{Chicago Which Hunt} \rightarrow Chicago\ wish\ hunt.$$

Just as the most common manner substitutes for stops were fricatives, so the most common manner substitutes for fricatives were stops. The targets in these errors were the fricatives /v,f,h/, all three relatively weak acoustically. The manner errors for target fricatives are given in Table 3.4.

In medial position, fricatives were most commonly misperceived as stops. One fricative, /ʃ/, was perceived as an affricate, /tʃ/. In final position, the only substitutes for target fricatives were stops.

3.1.3.2. Manner Errors for Resonants

Errors of target resonants were less frequent than errors of target obstruents. Almost half of the misperceptions resulted in obstruents, a much higher percentage than found for the reverse error. Errors occurred in all word positions, the most common being initial. Of the initial resonant errors, four involved /r/ as the target; all were perceived as /l/. There was only one example of the reverse error, /l/ perceived as /r/. Except for nasals, the resonants were typically perceived as resonants. Examples are given in Table 3.5.

There were approximately the same number of medial errors with resonant targets as there were initial errors with such targets. Five of the targets were lat-

TABLE 3.4   Manner Errors for Fricatives

<u>Initial fricatives perceived as stops</u>

He hasn't heard of any viable reasons → buyable reasons

who → goo

I don't like her black hat on the floor → black cat on the floor

Dad's Fad → bad

Joann Fokes → Cokes

greatest hits → greatest tits

little fritter → little critter

This is Six news at eight → This is Dick's news

<u>Other manner misperceptions of initial fricatives</u>

There's Jay → Where's Jay

having a nice van like that → nice man like that

Lasnik, Fiengo → Lasnik, Liengo

face → mace

<u>Medial fricatives</u>

There's a word I learned in high school—slovern → slobbern

How do you spell "savor"? → spell "saber"

When were you in the service? → circus

geyser → giger

cushion sole → kutchion sole

We need somebody with C's breathing in the building → breeding in the building

<u>Final fricatives</u>

How do you spell "diverse"? → divert

He understands move → mood

---

erals, and three of these were perceived as the voiced alveolar stop /d/. In final position, there were only three errors for resonant targets. Two targets were /l/, both perceived as /r/.

3.1.4. PLACE OF ARTICULATION SUBSTITUTIONS

Errors in the place of articulation of consonants were somewhat more common than manner errors. These could also involve errors of manner or voicing. Errors in place of articulation were most common in initial position, less so in final position, and least medially.

TABLE 3.5   Manner Errors for Resonants

Word-initial position

Target /l/

Lenny Willis returns the ball → Renny Willis

slip of the ear → snip of the ear

Target /r/

Groton Court → Gloton Court

I used to use that thing wrong → that thing long

That's the wrong time → long time

I have to say good-bye to the Frys → flies

Target glide

Yosemite → Dosemite

Target nasals

I'm getting married this Friday → buried this Friday

I'm trying to find some matches → some latches

Do you have a map of Mars? → of bars

ma'am → Pam

Medial resonants

Romy is pregnant again → Robbie

honors, awards → otter's awards

Hulon Willis → Huron Willis

mouli → moony

mouli → moody

the key to humility → to humidity

chameleon → comedian

Final resonants

I'd like a Krackle → cracker

hire some halls → some whores

Bob said it was noon → was nude

3.1.4.1. Place Errors of Labial Consonants

In initial position, only the two stops, the voiceless fricative /f/, and the nasal /m/ served as targets. Though most of the errors were exemplified by only a few tokens, the substitution of the voiceless velar stop /k/ for /p/ was the most common error. Further, velar consonants were the most common confusions for target labials. Misperceptions of labial targets were most frequent in final position; the labials were most commonly perceived as alveolars. The most frequent error target was the voiceless stop /p/. These data are given in Table 3.6.

After the misperception

grape arbor → grate arbor [as in "grate cheese"],

the listener was explicit about which word she had heard, *grate,* rather than the possible and perhaps more likely homophone, *great.* The listener's observation suggests that homophonous words with very different meanings have separate entries in the mental lexicon.

3.1.4.2. Place Errors for Dental and Alveolar Consonants

In initial position, each place of articulation error type occurred only once; the targets, however, were one of the two stops in all but one instance. As in initial position, each error type occurred only once in medial position, but the misperceived consonants were more varied.

The error

slip of the ear, *tlumbering* → *klumbering*

is the only token in the data set in which the target clearly violates English phonotactic constraints—there are no English words which begin with the consonant cluster /tl/. The speaker was explaining that one child misperception resulted in a non-English sequence and then gave the example. In spite of the introduction, the listener "corrected" the sequence to something more acceptable in English, *klumbering.*

The example

Patwin → Paʔwin

is the only error in which a non-English phoneme was reported. The alveolar stop of the target utterance may very well have been produced as an allophonic glottal stop; however, the listener, an anthropological linguist, either did not compensate for the allophonic variation or, if the target utterance did contain the stop /t/, substituted a non-English segment with which she was familiar in the context of other languages. Even though many of the speakers and listeners who have contributed to the data set are either familiar with other languages or bilingual, there is no other example of an adult perceiving a segment inappropriate to the language.

The five errors with alveolar targets in final position are also all unique. Only three consonants serve as targets, however: /t/, /θ/, and /n/. These data are included in Table 3.7.

TABLE 3.6   Misperceptions of Labial Targets

Initial position

Stops

porpoise lady → corpus lady

Councilman Portman → Cortman

I want to go see *Family Plot* → Family Klott

parrot → carrot

a poor house → a whore house

Dad, have you ever heard of blueing? → gluing

L D B D → L D D D

Tony Brazelton → Grazelton

Fricatives

phone → thone

Joann Fokes → Cokes

little fritter → little critter

Lasnik, Fiengo → Lasnik, Liengo

Nasals

I'm trying to find some matches → some latches

Medial position

Stops

Have her call Mike Rupright → Rutright

Epley → Ekley

Fricatives

The mining of Haiphong Harbor → Haithong Harbor

When were you in the service? → circus

Nasals

atmosphere → atnosphere

Final position

Stops

Where's the cap? → the cat

Stupid ship can't even survive a storm → stupid shit

Grape Nuts cereal → Great Nuts cereal

a star who does not use a professional claque → professional clack

They're going to shoot trap → to shoot track

(Continues)

TABLE 3.6   (*Continued*)

trap → track

Hi Rob → Hi Rod

grape arbor → grate arbor [as in "grate cheese"]

Fricatives

an afe → an eighth

They had a section for the deaf → for the death

I gave him a lift today → a list today

He understands move → mood

He understands move → mooth

Nasals

Key lime pie → key line pie

I tell MBA's what to do → NBA's

I read Coomb's paper last night → Kuhn's paper

3.1.4.3. Place Errors for Palatal and Velar Consonants

There was only two errors involving palatal targets:

> I wonder where Jimmy is going? → Timmy is going
> you are hearing Appalachian → hearing appellation.

Velar consonants served as targets for place errors rather often in initial and in final position, but there were no medial errors. Almost all of the errors involved the two stops; the nasal appeared as a place error target in only one token. The velars could apparently be misperceived as any of a number of consonants. The perceived consonants did not follow any noticeable pattern except that there were no voicing errors associated with final velars. The place errors for velar consonants are given in Table 3.8.

3.1.4.4. Errors for the Fricative /h/

Misperception of the fricative /h/ are given in Table 3.9. Two of the errors involved function words, hence may be misleading examples of phonetic errors. In the remaining three errors, /h/ was perceived as a stop.

3.1.5. ERRORS IN VOICING

Many of the manner and place errors have also involved errors in voicing. Voicing errors also occurred without concomitant place or manner misperceptions.

TABLE 3.7   Misperceptions of Dental/Alveolar Targets.

Initial position

She had on a trench suit → a French suit

I'll bet that'll be a teary program → cheery program

slip of the ear, *tlumbering* → *klumbering*

It's D R O I N O → B R O I N O

I stayed home and made some drapes → made some grapes

DC-9 → VC-9

There's Jay → Where's Jay

Medial position

booty → boolie

Patwin → Paʔwin

but next week I'll start using it pretty extensively → expensively

nasalization → navalization

geyser → giger

Lawnview → Longview

undramatical → ungrammatical

Final position

great → grape

at least this part of it → this park of it

Death in Venice → *Deaf in Venice*

Fifth Street → fifth string

Hey, man → Hey, ma'am

When you were little did you wear a corset, mom? → wear a corsep

The targets for such errors must, by necessity, be one of the obstruents. There were relatively few examples of voicing errors without any other misperception. The medial error

$$\text{traitor} \rightarrow \text{trader}$$

probably involved not so much a misperception as a misinterpretation of the target word. In all probability, the target was pronounced with an intervocalic flap. The listener interpreted the flap to represent a voiced rather than a voiceless alveolar stop. Voicing errors are given in Table 3.10.

TABLE 3.8   Misperceptions of Velar Targets

Initial position

What's a corpus lady? → porpoise lady

contextual cues → contextual pews

You're a goon brain → boon brain

Skandinavian languages → Standinavian

Don't forget the formula for the bridge cable → the bridge table

Captain Cook → Captain Hook

Karen → Darren

Kim Adams → Tim Adams

All of the members grew up in Philadelphia → threw up

Dr. Garber → Dr. Harber

Garnes → /dʒarnes/

Gary Dalton → very Dalton

Final position

The Coke went flying → the coat went flying

I want to get a Coke → get a coat

It looks like it's carved of teak → teeth

He must be a good Greek → good grief

professional claque → clap

We start our summer league tonight → summer leave

mag card → mad card

Long's → lawns

TABLE 3.9   Misperceptions of /h/

Does he come to class everyday? → Does she come to class

She doesn't know what he's doing? → know what she's doing

who → goo

I don't like her black hat on the floor → black cat on the floor

greatest hits → greatest tits

3.2. COMPLEX CONSONANT ERRORS

Consonant errors also occurred as part of complex errors. As in simple consonant errors, there were consonant substitutions, consonant loss, and consonant

TABLE 3.10   Errors in Voicing

Benny Pate → Benny Bate
traitor → trader
Will the class → Will the glass
Jim's out with his van → Jim's out with his fan
Her niece was in the hospital → Her knees
He is in the turkey-raising business. → turkey-racing business
Remember chain rule → Jane Rule
training for great book → grade book

additions. A misperception could exhibit more than one consonantal error type and be accompanied by other errors as well.

3.2.1. CONSONANT LOSS IN COMPLEX ERRORS

Of the consonant loss errors, there were approximately the same number of occurrences of loss of a singleton consonant and of loss of a consonant which was part of a cluster. Examples of loss of more than one consonant were rarer.

The position of loss of single consonants could be identified with reasonable certainty. Losses in initial position and in medial position were equally likely, but a much greater number of consonants were lost in final position. In addition, there were several examples of consonant loss in which the target was a function word. The preponderance of consonant loss in final position is consistent with simple consonant misperceptions.

3.2.1.1. Loss of Singleton Consonants

The examples of initial consonant loss are given in Table 3.11. The examples were fairly evenly divided between loss of obstruents and loss of resonants.

The examples of medial consonant loss are given in Table 3.12. Most commonly lost were obstruent targets, and the most common target was the voiced alveolar /d/. The loss of this consonant was often accompanied by loss of a syllable, as in

two models of speech perception → two miles.

Just as in medial position, in final position the most commonly affected consonants were obstruents (see Table 3.13).

The examples of consonant loss which affected primarily function words are given in Table 3.14. Many of these examples involve word boundary loss or

TABLE 3.11 Loss of a Single Consonant in Initial Position as Part of Complex Errors

Obstruent

Latvian festival → Latvian Eskimo

a process of residence selection → residence lection

something like *Poseidon Adventure* → like a silent adventure

Hi-C → ice tea

Nasal

Noel Matkin → Noam Atkin

Is he nasty? → Is he an ass?

Did you see my Nancy Reagan cards? → ANSI rating cards

Liquid or glide

rural free delivery → oral free delivery

still lousy → still assy

a U-Haul in front of us → an ink ball in front of us

Lisa has good taste → she has good taste

TABLE 3.12 Loss of a Single Consonant in Medial Position as Part of Complex Errors

Obstruent

Trudy → tree

on the middle staircase → the mill staircase

imagery → energy

How's David? → How's Gregg?

name is being withheld → repelled

Herbert H. Lehman College → Heritage Lehman College

a very exotic child → erotic child

two models of speech perception → two miles

She's working for the judiciary committee → for the Jewish charity committee

Liquid, glide or nasal

Mrs. Herrell → Mrs. Hill

The report is tolerable → is horrible

a Bulova watch → Bova watch

why I turned to Krylon → turned to crime

Janet Jackson → Chada Jackson

TABLE 3.13   Loss of a Single Consonant in Final Position as Part of Complex Errors

Obstruent

vowels excerpted from "heed" words → key words

Mandarin Chinese food → Mandarin Chinese flu

white roll → rye roll

foxglove → fox glow

I've never cooked anybody's goose → cooked anybody mousse

Anyone who thinks carob bean is a good substitute for chocolate is crazy → paraffin is a good
   substitute

Get a pill out → a pillow

portrait → poetry [speaker is British]

Nasal

I wouldn't eat at the restaurant in a motel unless it's snowing → unless it's smelly

citrus craving → citrus gravy

Try newspaper and a hot iron → hot air

from 180 some → for 180 some

The book I would recommend is by Paul Zemmlin → Zemler

Liquid or glide

Mar Dee Doll → Marty Dow

First stop of his four-nation tour → phonation tour

I feel secure → I disappear

reinterpretation. There was a tendency for a series of unstressed function words to be perceived as unstressed syllables belonging to a content word, as in the following example:

the floor of the house → the Florida house.

3.2.1.2. Loss of Consonants in Clusters

Consonants were lost as components of consonant clusters at a slightly higher rate than as singletons. The position in words of affected consonants was proportionately the same for singletons as for consonants in clusters in that loss was equally likely in initial clusters and medial clusters but more common in final clusters. Just as for singleton consonants, final position was the favored environment for consonant loss. The examples of consonant loss in initial clusters are given in Table 3.15. The majority of lost consonants were liquids or glides, the second segment of consonant clusters.

TABLE 3.14   **Consonant Loss in Function Words**

I have them do out of class writing → auto class writing

the floor of the house → the Florida house

with less than two weeks to go → less than two weeks ago

When were you here? → Why were you here?

I'm going to try to get it towed → to get a toad

I have to eat too → I have eighty-two

I'll catch my breath here → my brushup

missed the news → must a snoozed

It will be how many years? → It will be twenty years

I think I see a place → I think I see his face

fruits and vegetables → prudent vegetables

no she isn't → no shitting

someone else isn't neat this morning → is in heat this morning

I got to sleep at a decent hour → to sleep at least an hour

with drugs → at stud

Polly played with Tom → polyp laden /θam/

All examples of consonant loss in medial clusters are given in Table 3.16. Obstruents were the most commonly affected consonants, with few nasals and fewer liquids or glides serving as targets. Examples such as

I have a dental appointment → a dinner appointment
mental science → middle science

are very similar to nasal plus obstruent clusters misperceptions in simpler errors. It seems that the listeners failed to compensate for the reduced clusters.

Of the many examples of consonant loss in final position, the majority involved target obstruents. These typically occurred in a cluster consisting of two obstruents or the liquid /r/ followed by an obstruent. The examples of these errors are given in Table 3.17.

Table 3.18 gives examples of consonant loss in which the relationships between the target and the misperception are complex though they seem to involve the loss of few consonants.

Table 3.19 gives examples in which the relationship between the target utterance and the misperception was difficult to specify. In all cases, more than one consonant was lost. Sometimes it was not at all clear which consonants were lost and which involved a substitution. In most of these examples, the

TABLE 3.15   Consonant is Lost in an Initial Cluster

Obstruent

Blair → Ware

Bruce is going to sing → Ruth is going to sing

Skippers' Treat → trick or treat

stomach flu → summit flu

Flum → mom

Liquid or glide

Greektown → Wheattown

Claude → Rod

trained at Cornell → chained at Cornell

grant → camp

quiet → buy it

we had a representative of the preschool come → of the Peace Corps

lunch in a huge cafeteria → in a Jewish cafeteria

Anne Schwarz → had on shorts

look at the cloud cover → card cover

---

misperception appeared to be confined to one word. In a few, a word or more was lost as part of the misperception.

3.2.2. CONSONANT ADDITIONS IN COMPLEX ERRORS

On the basis of the frequency of occurrence, consonant additions and consonant loss were about equally likely. About two-thirds of the errors involved the addition of a single consonant, while the remainder involved the addition of more than one consonant, sometimes in quite complicated relationships. In addition, there were several examples of additions which appeared to affect primarily function words.

When it was possible to identify one added consonant with reasonable certainty, initial and final additions were more common than medial additions.

The initial consonant addition errors are given in Table 3.20. The majority of the added consonants were stops, sometimes added preceding a vowel, as in the example

I kept an eye on the Big Dipper last night → I kept denying the Big Dipper.

TABLE 3.16   Consonant Loss in Medial Clusters

Obstruents

seismology → psychology

nonaccessible storage → nonaggressible storage

inflection → inflation

interestin' → Enarson

I am a wombat → a woman

interview → ennerview

I have a dental appointment → a dinner appointment

Bette Midler → Pat Miller

movement → Newton

Nasals

a diet to increase my sexual potency → to appease my sexual potency

meet Mr. Anderson → Mr. Edison

Cathy needs change for the laundry → for the lottery

mental science → middle science

Liquids or glides

Nelson → Neusa

We're going to Xenia → to Adena

Sometimes the stop was added preceding a liquid or glide, creating an initial cluster:

raised chocolate donut → glazed chocolate.

There were only three clear cases of fricatives added in initial position. In the example

It depends on the Finns → on the spin

the listener misperceived the target word *Finns* as having an initial /s/; the /f/ was perceived as a stop, perhaps influenced by the fact that /sp/ is a common initial consonant cluster whereas /sf/ is extremely rare. Two examples may have resulted from interpreting the relationship between a fricative and a word boundary inappropriately:

Dennis Molfese brought all his students → Dennis Smallpiece
I know what happened to our ice, Andy → to high Sandy

TABLE 3.17   Consonant Loss in a Final Cluster

Obstruent

round trip → one trip

It depends on the Finns → on the spin

an exam at Kent State → Wayne State

Don't make it a horse story → a horror story

My handout isn't as good as I hoped it would be → I told it would be

giving an award → giving an oral

one of the court poets → the poor poets

He got ten years in prison → tenure in prison

It's in a real forest → a real farce

I want to go out to a state park → to a steak bar

What Phil Morse is going to do → what Fillmore is going to do

How does the west look? → the bus look

IREX → I was

they're all nuts → all nice

cracked → track

It's typed → his type

Room 260 is locked → is a lot

I'm covered with chalk dust → with chocolate

A friend of ours is having a lung removed → is having alumni move

It will be done next year → in six years

I just like it → I dislike it

with drugs → at stud

Nasal

important → imported

a slant board → a sled board

teaching summer quarter is worth two-ninths → is worth two nights

book on primate infants → primate incest

I tripped on a tent pole → tadpole

Liquid or glide

too close to melt → to mouth

no shit, Little Beaver → no shittling beaver

How about your tires? → your title

an honors political science course → honest political science course

---

TABLE 3.18   Consonant Loss is Involved in Complex Relationships.

barbell set → bord la sell

he and Annie's father → he and his father

an errand to run near High Street → to run on new High Street

I didn't have to wear a coat → to work

You've got all the books you need for the time being → for your typing

I know what happened to our ice, Andy → to high Sandy

the anechoic chamber → the ambionic chamber

four wheat pennies → four weekends

living with a coach → women who coach

they took footprints when you're born → they took footprints in the dorm

I need to talk to him → I need to calculate

a linguini is a noodle → a lean Wheatie is a noodle

the Clemency Information Center → the Columbus Information Center

Mary, would you like some tea with this? → to eat with us

constraint-based phonology → straight-faced phonology

In the first example, the fricative was distributed between both words; in the second, it began the second word rather than ending the first.

The examples of identifiable consonant addition in medial position are given in Table 3.21. Most commonly, the added consonant was a liquid or a stop.

A large proportion of consonant additions in final position involved obstruent plus nasal sequences. In half the examples, a nasal was added preceding an obstruent, as in

I don't fight for causes → find for causes.

In the other half of the examples, a stop was added following a nasal, as in

the old creek inn was deserted → creek end was deserted.

Both of these patterns suggest that the listeners were using knowledge of English phonology to compensate for supposedly reduced nasal plus obstruent clusters. All examples of final consonant additions are given in Table 3.22.

The examples in which consonant addition was associated with readjustements of function words are given in Table 3.23.

TABLE 3.19   More Than One Consonant Is Lost

Less than a word is lost

John Eulenberg → John Gilbert

RP-ized → RPI

glottal wave of the deaf → auto wave of the deaf

the *Edmond Fitzgerald* → Edna Fitzgerald

tendency → Tennessee

The bottom's all covered with eels → the bob

my coffee cup refilled → my coffee cup fell

accidents → actions

That's not a part of the remedial program → the reading program

front vowels occur only in words → front vowels are Kyrolean words

German's looking for a room → Jim's looking

I take a couple of Anacin → a cup of acid

Jane Kollaritsch → Jane Clark

change for a dollar → exchange a dollar

those shoes → oh shoot

West State Street → West Eight Street

I'm conking out → coffee out

It'll be a confusing weekend → You're confusing weekends

We were in Amherst together → enamorous together

catch a five-pounder → catch a flounder

Olga's son → the sun

Star Fire → /sta fa/

A word or more is lost

just bisecting lines → just bicycling

an apartment for a hundred and ten a month → for ten a month

You're not wearing one → not married

I was running around after a slide projector → after a sniper

kills germs where they grow → kills germs with egg roll

This goes through forty-eight → through Fourier

I didn't have to wear a coat → to work

It will be how many years? → It will be twenty years

the meaning of the word average has changed over the years → the mean of the average

TABLE 3.20   Consonant Addition in Initial Position as Part of Complex Errors

Obstruent

raised chocolate donut → glazed chocolate

It depends on the Finns → on the spin

He could run his son → burn his son

Astrid Gilberto → bastard Gilberto

my three-ninety class → my three-D night class

it would hurt it → it would pervert it

white → quiet

I kept an eye on the Big Dipper last night → I kept denying the Big Dipper

Dennis Molfese brought all his students → Dennis Smallpiece

eat a Maple Leaf wiener → a make-believe wiener

Hi-C → ice tea

I know what happened to our ice, Andy → to high Sandy

osill → ass hole

setting up of time → studying of time

Eddie Hall → Betty Hall

East Knox local schools → these Knox local schools

Nasal

We will just arrest him → molest him

evolution of tense systems → of intense systems

we eat at eight → we needed eight

structure, style, and usage → instruct your style and usage

Liquid or glide

I'm serious → I'm furious

the urn is finished → the urine is finished

foods → fruits

Isn't this nice for a border? → a quarter

Mandarin Chinese food → Mandarin Chinese flu

bubonic → Blue Bonnet

How's David? → How's Gregg?

there up ahead → clear up ahead

catch a five-pounder → catch a flounder

TABLE 3.21   Addition of a Consonant in Medial Position as Part of Complex Errors

Obstruent

the pony league → pointer league

psychic → psychotic

roll up the back window → patrol the back window

I just got back from Dennison → back from dentist

How do you spell "Cochran" → spell "popcorn"

it will be a tenting situation → tempting situation

red spire pears → red spider pears

Nasal

Bikerton → Pinkerton

orgasm → organism

Garnes → Garmens

Is that margarine? → Is that Mondrian?

doggie → donkey

fresh artillery fire in Croatia → French artillery fire

Liquid or glide

I found it → Icelandic

It's that lousy atomic bread I can't stand → Italian bread

the habitat → the havercamp

a fancy seductive letter → a fancy structive letter

Falstaff → Flagstaff

we offered six → we Alfred six

erudite → area dried

matches → mattress

Finally, there were many examples in which more than one consonant was added. In some of these errors, the relationships was clear but involved numerous changes, as in the examples

I'm going up for my office hours → for my vodka sours
He doesn't mow his own lawn → He doesn't blow his own horn.

In other cases, the relationship between the target utterance and the misperception was complex. For example,

Anne Schwarz → had on shorts
She's working for the judiciary committee → for the Jewish charity committee.

TABLE 3.22.   Addition of a Consonant in Final Position as Part of Complex Errors

Obstruent

Well, I'll sit here and peck away some more → decolate some more

an honors political science course → honest political science course

she's ripe → she's raped

Let me now try to develop this point → not try to develop

Penn State → Kent State

I have to go to the moon at six → to the mint at six

the old creek inn was deserted → creek end was deserted

felicity conditions → ballistic conditions

Dover sole → Dover salad

It's made with ham bone → with hand bone

overcorrection → overt correction

on an island with a moat surrounding it → with moats surrounding it

a loose end in this problem → a leaf's end

She lives in that same area → saint area

the anechoic chamber → the ambionic chamber

Nasal

I don't fight for causes → find for causes

a fresh salad → a French salad

my appointment was rather long → running long

A lot of kids are going to Oswego → to Sweden

SWAT leader → swamp leaper

I was through on a bus → I was thrown off a bus

spun toffee → fun stocking

Chris Evert at Wimbledon → Prince Edward

We must get some sealing tape → ceiling paint

Christy Bridge → Christy Grinch

assigned to the grad coordinator → grant coordinator

Liquid or glide

Wardhaugh → Wardhol

the PON → the PLN

Do you want me to recite? → to recycle

How about your tires? → your title

Mad River township → Madrigal township

(*Continues*)

TABLE 3.22   *(Continued)*

The king spoke in a flawed style → florid style

bookshop → bookshelf

something like *Poseidon Adventure* → like a silent adventure

To go for Mike → Nicole for Mike

Harms → Harlens

TABLE 3.23   Addition of a Consonant Affects a Function Word

---

hypnotic age regression → hypnotic aid to regression

In four to six months we'll get a house → four to six marks will get you a house

I think I see a place → I think I see his face

It's a dollar a quarter → It's a dollar and a quarter

You swallowed a watermelon → you smiled at a watermelon

Ann was afraid to go → afraid to do it

an errand to run near High Street → to run on New High Street

a purse and a billfold → a personal billfold

Coke and a Danish → coconut Danish

kills germs where they grow → kills germs with egg roll

I don't think of the bass as a solo instrument → as so low an instrument

Sara Garnes and Ilse → Sara Garnes Nielsen

Jefferson Starship → Jeffers and starship

I get to leave this place → I can't believe this place

All examples which involve the addition of several consonants are given in Table 3.24.

3.2.3. CONSONANT SUBSTITUTIONS IN COMPLEX ERRORS

In the simplest examples of these errors, only one consonant substitution took place. Of these, twice as many affected obstruents as resonants.

3.2.3.1. Substitutions for Obstruents

The substitutions for stops are given in in Table 3.25. In most of these errors, the target was either initial or medial and there were more voiceless targets than

TABLE 3.24   Addition of Several Consonants in Complex Errors

I'm going up for my office hours → for my vodka sours

Couldn't you say that was an SPC? → was misperceived?

Can I saw? → crawl

Wardhaugh → warthog

My handout isn't as good as I hoped it would be → I told it would be

usual grace period → illegal grace period

SUNOCO has a battery → snorkel has a battery

myo-functional therapy → mild functional therapy

two hundred hours → two hundred dollars

Finn → friend

a diet to increase my sexual potency → to appease my sexual potency

Hello, big boy → big Bart

Dennison → dentist

We're going to stay in Tebins → in tenements

front vowels occur only in words → front vowels are Kyrolean words

It will be done next year → in six years

We got our task force grant → our tennis court grant

This friend of ours who visited → of ours is an idiot

I love you and my baby → I love you. You are my baby

change for a dollar → exchange a dollar

Anne Schwarz → had on shorts

Viennese → Vietnamese

the radio on → the regular one

He doesn't mow his own lawn → He doesn't blow his own horn

a U-Haul in front of us → an ink ball in front of us

missed the news → must a snoozed

get me a mine → get me some wine

Is that home baked? → Is that hard to bake?

That's the kind he used before → used in the Air Force

It'll be a confusing weekend → You're confusing weekends

I'll catch my breath here → catch my breakfast

That's a good way to get your car door taken off → your carburetor taken off

I got to sleep at a decent hour → to sleep at least an hour

I'm horny → It's morning

choose any nineteen → two seventy nineteen

(Continues)

TABLE 3.24   *(Continued)*

I don't think we could afford to bring him here → could get a Ford to bring him here

Louisiana → New Zealand

She's working for the Judiciary Committee → for the Jewish charity committee

I need air → I need ear muffs

Do you have any Wite-Out? → white album

---

voiced. In medial position, the most common targets for misperceptions were alveolar stops, which were probably produced as flaps. Undoubtedly, neutralization of the targets tended to promote these errors.

The misperceptions of fricatives and affricates are given in Table 3.26. The errors which affected function words are given separately. In one of these errors,

We had this appointment . . . → disappointment,

the listener interrupted the speaker in midsentence, showing concern for whatever problem or misfortune the speaker was going to describe. This interruption supports the idea that speech understanding is extremely rapid; listeners do not lag behind speakers by more than a fraction of a word.

The remaining target fricatives were initial or medial, with only two misperceived targets in final position. There were few misperceptions of target affricates.

3.2.3.2. Substitutions for Resonants

The errors for target nasal consonants are given in Table 3.27. By far the most common position for errors was final, and in this position the velar nasal /ɔ/ was the most common target.

Errors for liquids and glides are given in Table 3.28. There were few errors in this category. The most common target for misperceptions was the consonantal /r/ in medial and final position.

The error

barrel → bottle

is unusual. The speaker had a pronounced East European accent and produced the medial /r/ as a flap, as a rhotic would be pronounced in her native language. Apparently, the listener followed the phonetic information and interpreted the flap as a /t/ rather than compensating for the accented English.

TABLE 3.25   Substitutions for Stop Consonants in Complex Errors

Initial position

pull course → cool course

Pier One Imports → beer wine imports

in different positions → indifferent physicians

PEO → BO

back window → tack one doe

she wants to be a teacher → she wants me to teach her

Maybe we ought to give up descriptive linguistics → give up the script of linguistics

He's Snoopy in disguise → in the skies

cloudy → ploddy

Givon → pavane

Many a father has been greeted by a roller skate → created by a roller skate

Dec man tomorrow → Pacman tomorrow

Polly played with Tom → polyp laden /θam/

attorney Larry L. Rowe → a dirty Larry L. Rowe

Chris De Pino → Christofino

constraint-based phonology → straight-faced phonology

Medial position

wrapping service → wrecking service

shabby furniture → Chevy furniture

lighter → ladder

your ladder → your letter

assorted → a sordid

See the giant meadow muffin → metal muffin

the Codofil people → the colorful people

Levi Jackson → Levi Jetson

I think it's a penguin → a pink one

Did you see my Nancy Reagan cards? → ANSI rating cards

Eddie Hall → Betty Hall

doggie → donkey

Riga → Eurika

Final position

illegible → illogical

got a reaction → gonorrhea action

parachute → pair of shoes

(Continues)

TABLE 3.25   *(Continued)*

Legg and Davis → Leggett Davis

I have a weed trimmer → I have a weak tremor

one cup of weak coffee → one Cocoa Wheat Puff

Thai food → typhoon

stomach flu → summit flu

fresh artillery fire in Croatia → French artillery fire

Janet Jackson → Chada Jackson

I tripped on a tent pole → tadpole

I lighted → I like it

3.2.3.3. Special Cases of Substitutions

There were a small number of rather specialized errors which deserve separate mention.

First, there were repetitive errors, i.e., those in which the same consonant was misperceived in the same way more than once. The examples of this error type are given in Table 3.29.

Secondly, there were fusion errors—misperceptions in which two target consonants appear to be blended into one, since traces of both are present in the misperception. Half of these errors involved the sequence /tr/ being perceived as an affricate, an error with a reasonable phonetic basis since the /r/ in this position is typically partially devoiced and produced with considerable noisy airflow. These errors were the inverse of an error such as

matches → mattress.

All examples of fusion errors are given in Table 3.30.

3.3. GENERAL PROPERTIES OF CONSONANT ERRORS

Simple consonant errors could readily be described in traditional phonetic terms as misperceptions in manner, place, or voicing. Even many errors which occurred as part of complex misperceptions could also be characterized in the same way. Zwicky and Zwicky (1986) comment that phonological relationships showing perceptual similarity are quite general, also characterizing puns.

TABLE 3.26   Substitution Errors for Fricatives and Affricates

In function words

He's out supervising the back hoe → supervising tobacco

That's a good idea for the future → What's a good idea

Did you put the food out for him? → for them

So you're going to be there two years in a row? → to be edder two years

We had this appointment . . . → disappointment

the OED → DOED

Worse'n that → Where's Annette

Mary, would you like some tea with this → to eat with us

Initial position

Exotic birds from far-off lands are fascinating → are assassinating

Clara W I E C K → W I Z K

I bought a slide hammer → slide camera

Hyman → Lehmann

Haggai's thesis → the guy's thesis

Flum → mom

I didn't know he had a big fancy car like that → big country car

Medial position

five-sixths of all conversions in the church → of all conversations

savor → sable

enshrinee's dinner → Chinese dinner

He's a fiscal liberal → physical liberal

cathedral → gazebo

IMSAI → INZAI

Final position

foxglove → fox globe

off → up

Affricates

toast and jelly → toast and chili

trying to get over being chairman → being German

It's called *The Absence of a Cello* → *The Absence of Othello*

converge en masse → conversion mass

Geez, really? → Disraeli

AHA → AAJ

Janet Jackson → Chada Jackson

TABLE 3.27 Errors for Target Nasal Consonants

Initial position

I'm staying near O'Hare → more O'Hare

on neurolinguistics → on zero linguistics

nose and eyes → Molson Ice

Medial position

her fiance's Canadian → comedian

meaningfulness → mean influence

IMSAI → INZAI

the anechoic chamber → the ambionic chamber

Final position

Who's calling? → Who's Colleen?

loan word → long word

I already claimed it → cleaned it

a big heavy ring → a big heavy rain

It's going to ring in a minute → rain in a minute

The beings on Mars have destroyed our latest spacecraft → the beans

Wouldn't she look good with a ring in her nose → oregano nose

He runs a driving school → a drive-in school

I'm not American → not a miracle

TABLE 3.28 Substitution Errors for Liquids and Glides

Substitutions for /r/

boiled these pearls in cherry preserves → in chili preserves

passed with a four → with a full

Westover → Westoak

I know where the place is → what the place is

barrel → bottle

Substitutions for /l/

a small computer → a smoke computer

Texas Women's University → Texas Lumens University

Substitutions for /w/

How's your work going? → book going

sewing it → selling it

TABLE 3.29   Repetitive Consonant Errors

What does *vivace* /vivas/ mean? → What does *bibas* mean?

gallons and gallons of coffee → jallons and jallons of coffee

We eat at eight → we needed eight

heart to heart → hard to hard

TABLE 3.30   Consonant Fusion Errors

't shows → Joe's

everybody's human → everybody's showman

trained at Cornell → chained at Cornell

boustrophed[on]ic → Posturepedic

I'm on a trip now → a chip one

We are not using the accident rates yet → not using the accident rate shit

However, at least some of the consonant errors exhibited a relatively global similarity between the target utterance and the misperception. These errors suggest that speech perception operates as much on the basis of partial global similarities as on the basis of segmental identity.

Consonant misperceptions involving substitution tended to be more common in the initial position then elsewhere, approximately in a 2:1 ratio. The most likely explanation for this finding rests on the observation that listeners can identify a word from partial phonetic information. For example, Grosjean (1980) presented word fragments to listeners beginning with the initial few milliseconds. He found that listeners proposed candidate words before they heard all relevant phonetic information. The listeners whose errors contributed to the misperceptions were also probably responding on the basis of partial information in arriving at a word, but their analysis of the initial portion of the word was incorrect. Consequently, the word which suggested itself to them was also incorrect. Since analysis of the remainder of a word would be less crucial for word identity, a correct word beginning would lead to an appropriately recognized word much more frequently.

Perceptual loss of consonants was most common in the final position. Word-final consonants tend to be weakly articulated and consonants in final clusters are often reduced, so listeners may be less attentive to final than to initial consonants. It may also be that listeners are less expectant of further phonetic material when they have recognized a word. This may very well be the explanation for errors such as *tray* for *train* and *car* for *cart*.

Listeners clearly relied on phonological knowledge in identifying words. Overwhelmingly, misperceptions result in well-formed phonological words appropriate to English. With one exception, all perceived consonants and vowels were members of the segment inventory of English. All perceived words matched English phonotactic constraints.

Listeners apparently used phonological knowledge to compensate for fast speech and dialect characteristics of speakers. Sometimes a reduced form of a target word lead to a misperception when listeners simply followed the phonetic representation. In other cases, listeners compensated inappropriately for reduced forms or dialect differences, reporting segments that were neither said nor intended.

CHAPTER 4

Misperceptions of the Shape of Words

[P]honological constraints are . . . made of rubber, not of steel.
—Charles F. Hockett (1967)

In contrast to simple local misperceptions, complex misperceptions often resulted in changes in the overall shape of words and even phrases or sentences. Properties which may be misperceived are the stress patterns of words, the number of syllables within a word or a phrase, and the placement of word boundaries. The order of segments and syllables within a word may also be misperceived. The most revealing way of describing complex misperceptions is to consider how the phonological shape of the misperception matched or failed to match the target utterance.

4.1. STRESS PATTERN

The role of stress in word recognition in English is not entirely clear. On the one hand, the stress pattern appears to be clearly linked to the overall shape of a word and therefore would seem to provide essential information for its recognition. This evaluation of the role of stress is supported, for example, by the tip-of-the-tongue phenomenon in which a word that a subject has "on the tip of his/her tongue" tends to match the stress pattern of the target word (Brown & McNeill, 1966). On the other hand, Cutler (1986) has suggested that stress is not a part of the code used for word recognition in English. She bases this conclusion on her finding that minimal pairs based on stress patterns, such as FORbear vs. forBEAR, behave like homophones. The same conclusion has been reached by Small, Simon, and Goldberg (1988), who found, in a word recognition task, that listeners' reaction times were equal for words which were correctly stressed and for words which exhibited a stress pattern inappropriate to the context provided by the sentence. From this point of view, stressed or strong syllables may aid in segmenting the stream of speech but not be used in accessing words in the mental lexicon.

In our data, there were few examples of a misperceived stress pattern. Seven of the misperceptions maintained the same number of syllables between the target utterance and the misperception, while the remainder involved either an addition or a loss of a syllable. These are given in Table 4.1.

TABLE 4.1   Misperceived Stress Patterns

Same syllable number

giving an award → giving an oral

Who's calling? → Who's Colleen?

usual grace period → illegal grace period

conditions are almost right → Hendersons are almost right

roll up the back window → patrol the back window

Geez, really? → Disraeli

no bullshit exams → noble shit exams

the Clemency Information Center → the Columbus Information Center

Change in syllable number

Five-sixths of all conversions in the church → of all conversations

portrait → poetry [speaker is British]

John Eulenberg → John Gilbert

Sunoco has a battery → snorkel has a battery

I'm in the Political Science Department → pickle science department

psychic → psychotic

front vowels occur only in words → front vowels are Kyrolean words

I have to eat too → I have eighty-two

my three-ninety class → my three-D night class

Louisiana → New Zealand

The misperception data do not resolve the issues concerning the role of stress in word recognition. Because the number of affected words was relatively small, it is difficult to dismiss stress completely as irrelevant to word recognition. The errors suggest that there was a tendency to make errors toward the more typical or expected English pattern. For example, *patrol* as a misperception of *roll up* is stressed on the second syllable, as is typical of verbs, and *oral* as a misperception of *award* has first syllable stress, as is typical of nouns. However, stress errors did not lead to the more typical stress pattern in all cases.

4.2. CHANGES IN SYLLABLE NUMBER

In the set of complex misperceptions, a large number involved a change in the number of syllables between the spoken target and its misperceived version. In the typical case, only one syllable was either added or lost. The additions and the deletions of portions of words were approximately equal in number. There were only a few examples of more than one syllable being added or lost. Among the one-syllable additions and deletions, there were several examples in which the listener reported hearing an additional word or failed to hear a word. Typically a function word was affected. These seem to deserve a separate classification.

An interesting characteristic of some of the misperceptions involving the number of syllables is that it is not always obvious which syllable has been affected. There are certainly clear cases, such as the following examples:

> Don't make it a horse story → a horror story
> The Ascent of Man → the scent of man.

In the first example the mismatch is clearly a two-syllable misperception, *horror,* of the one syllable *horse,* while in the second example the first syllable of *ascent* is missing. But other examples involve misperceptions in which traces of most or all syllables are present but the total number of syllables differs from target to misperception. Two examples of such cases, which are relatively plentiful, follow:

> We're going to stay in Tebins → in tenements
> Louisiana → New Zealand.

A practical implication from this observation is that the classification of misperceptions by position—whether the added or lost syllable is initial, medial, or final—has to be taken as tentative, a judgment call. A more interesting implication is for word recognition. It certainly seems likely that word recognition is being accomplished by means of fragmentary, partial phonological representations; these are not necessarily sequentially ordered segments, but rather seem to resemble features or properties distributed throughout a large part of a word.

4.2.1. One Syllable Is Added

Most commonly, a syllable was added as part of a lexical item, though in some instances word boundaries were also affected. Typically, the added syllable was unstressed. The extraneous syllable was most likely to be word final; word initial and word medial extraneous syllables were less common. Some of the syllable additions probably have phonetic explanations. In several varieties of American English, word-final /l/ and /r/ may have one-syllable or two-syllable pronunciations. In examples such as

That's an *L* → an *A–O*
mail → mayo

the speaker may have pronounced the sequence /ɛl/ as two syllables, with a final syllabic consonant. The listener interpreted the pronunciation as a vocalic syllable. This explanation would be appropriate for a number of final syllable additions when the target word ends in /l/ or /r/. The examples of one-syllable additions classified according to position are given in Table 4.2.

4.2.2. One Syllable Is Lost

The distribution of omitted syllables was approximately the same as that of added syllables. The most common word position in which subjects were likely to add a syllable was the final position. Addition of syllables at the initial and medial positions was less common. Most of the deleted syllables would be very short in casual speech, sometimes less than 25 ms. in duration (see Fokes & Bond, 1989), so perhaps it is not surprising that listeners would fail to detect them on occasion. Since an extraneous syllable can be perceived on the basis of dialect variation in the way final /l/ and /r/ are treated, a syllable can also be lost on this basis, as in the following example:

Mrs. Herrell → Mrs. Hill.

In addition, weakly stressed final vowels might be perceived as consonantal for essentially similar reasons, as in

myo-functional therapy → mild functional therapy
about some follow-up → some foul-up.

TABLE 4.2   One Syllable Is Added

Added syllable is initial

exotic birds from far-off lands are fascinating → are assassinating

evolution of tense systems → of intense systems

the most literate → most illiterate

Leena → Elena

We're going to Xenia → to Adena

it would hurt it → it would pervert it

So you're going to be there two years in a row? → to be edder two years

structure, style, and usage → instruct your style and usage

Riga → Eurika

Added syllable is medial

five-sixths of all conversions in the church → of all conversations

portrait → poetry [speaker is British]

Cathy needs change for the laundry → for the lottery

Many a father has been greeted by a roller skate → created by a roller skate

psychic → psychotic

We're going to stay in Tebins → in tenements

He's a fiscal liberal → physical liberal

We were in Amherst together → enamorous together

Dec writer → decorator

your nation → urination

got a reaction → gonorrhea action

erudite → area dried

wrangler → regular

Added syllable is final

They're getting off their course → their chorus

two hundred hours → two hundred dollars

That's an L → an A–O

I bought a slide hammer → slide camera

lunch in a huge cafeteria → in a Jewish cafeteria

Dover sole → Dover salad

The king spoke in a flawed style → florid style

Do you want me to recite? → to recycle

Don't make it a horse story → a horror story

(*Continues*)

TABLE 4.2 *(Continued)*

Does he have any hair? → any higher

His name is Swain → Swaney

How about your tires? → your title

The urn is finished → the urine is finished

You can spend a mint eating → you can spend a minute

We got our task force grant → our tennis court grant

the paramour → the power mower

Do you have any Wite-Out? → white album

white → quiet

She's working for the Judiciary Committee → for the Jewish charity committee

mail → mayo

Those are nice pants → nice peanuts

Harms → Harlens

In addition, there was a tendency for two adjacent vowels to be blended into one syllable:

no she isn't → no shitting
The beings on Mars have destroyed our latest spacecraft → the beans on Mars
I teach speech science → speech signs.

The example

> a fancy seductive letter → a fancy structive letter

supports the strong tendency for misperceptions to be phonologically well formed. When the listener failed to detect the short vowel of the initial syllable of *seductive,* he interpreted the stop following /s/ as voiceless, appropriate to English phonotactic constraints. The examples of syllable loss classified by syllable position are given in Table 4.3.

A very clear example of phonological reduction leading to perceptual loss of a syllable is provided by the token

> support services → sport services.

In all probability, the speaker produced a very short, indistinct vowel in the first syllable and the listener did not compensate for the reduction. There are no clear examples of the reverse error—perceptually adding a syllable in order to compensate for a supposed phonological reduction.

TABLE 4.3   One Syllable Is Lost

Lost syllable is initial

The Ascent of Man → the scent of man

a phonetic explanation of phonology by Ohala → by Halle

my coffee cup refilled → my coffee cup fell

a process of residence selection → residence lection

a fancy seductive letter → a fancy structive letter

A lot of kids are going to Oswego → to Sweden

a Bulova watch → Bova watch

catch a five-pounder → catch a flounder

no she isn't → no shitting

Do you know *New Dimensions?* → know nude mentions

constraint-based phonology → straight-faced phonology

enshrinees' dinner → Chinese dinner

office of public occasions → office of publications

support services → sport services

Lost syllable is medial

myo-functional therapy → mild functional therapy

the report is tolerable → is horrible

John Eulenberg → John Gilbert

about some follow-up → some foul-up

accidents → actions

Denison → dentist

I just got back from Denison → back from dentist

Louisiana → New Zealand

representational → reputational

Lost syllable is final

low visibility → lovas

SUNOCO has a battery → snorkel has a battery

This is mystery dressing → Mr. Dressing

Mrs. Herrell → Mrs. Hill

I teach speech science → speech signs

Sara → sir

Two models of speech perception → two miles

What's another word for menorah → for manure

(Continues)

TABLE 4.3   (*Continued*)

I say crayon → crown

It's in a real forest → a real farce

Westover → Westoak

The bottom's all covered with eels → the bob's all covered

plant dying → plant dung

felicity conditions → ballistic conditions

the Arabs and the Israelis → herbs and the Israelis

on the middle staircase → the mill staircase

He and Annie's father → he and his father

Why I turned to Krylon → turned to crime

The beings on Mars have destroyed our latest spacecraft → the beans

Trudy → tree

German's looking for a room → Jim's looking

How's David? → How's Gregg?

no shit, Little Beaver → no shittling beaver

You've got all the books you need for the time being → for your typing

Olga's son → the sun

four wheat pennies → four weekends

one cup of weak coffee → one cocoa Wheat Puff

Do you have any aspirin? → have a napkin

4.2.3. MORE THAN ONE SYLLABLE IS AFFECTED

Of the examples in which more than one syllable was affected, the majority involved loss of syllables. In only four errors were extraneous syllables added. As best as can be determined from examining the match between the targets and the misperceptions, all the added syllables were unstressed. However, unstressed as well as stressed or potentially stressed syllables could be lost, leaving some of their consonants behind. These data are given in Table 4.4.

There is a noticeable asymmetry in the position in which syllables are added or deleted. About twice as many final syllables are added or deleted as initial or medial syllables. Part of the explanation is undoubtedly phonetic, based on variation in the pronunciation of final liquids and nasals as well as on a tendency to pronounce the final portions of words indistinctly. Sometimes sequences of vowels or liquids may also receive indistinct pronunciation, as in

The beings on Mars have destroyed our latest spacecraft → the beans.

TABLE 4.4   More Than One Syllable Is Affected

Loss

an apartment for a hundred and ten a month → for ten a month

I'm in the political science department → pickle science department

That's not a part of the remedial program → the reading program

I take a couple of Anacin → a cup of acid

Jane Kollaritsch → Jane Clark

It'll be a confusing weekend → You're confusing weekends

I didn't have to wear a coat → to work

I was running around after a slide projector → after a sniper

Additions

That's the kind he used before → used in the Air Force

That's a good way to get your car door taken off → your carburetor taken off

choose any nineteen → two seventy nineteen

orgasm → organism

On occasion, it appears that a listener has recoverd a word and simply does not attend to further phonetic information, as in the misperception

> This is mystery dressing → Mr. Dressing.

But because portions of missing syllables are often perceptually present, syllable loss can not always be attributed to closing off a lexical search.

4.2.4. A Word Is Added

Table 4.5 lists all examples of syllable addition in which the added element is a word rather than part of a word. In only one of these the added word is a content word:

> I need air → I need earmuffs.

All other added words are function words which seem to be required for the perceived utterance to be grammatical. The most likely explanation is that the listener has misperceived some portion of the utterance which would lead to an ungrammatical string if there were no other changes. For example, the misperception

> It's a dollar a quarter → It's a dollar and a quarter,

would lead to *It's a dollar and quarter* if the listener merely interpreted the article *a* as the word *and* without further adjustments. Apparently, listeners edited

TABLE 4.5   Added Element Is a Word

In four to six months we'll get a house → four to six marks will get you a house

this friend of ours who visited → of ours is an idiot

I love you and my baby → I love you. You are my baby.

Anne Schwarz → had on shorts

It's a dollar a quarter → It's a dollar and a quarter

hypnotic age regression → hypnotic aid to regression

You swallowed a watermelon → You smiled at a watermelon

Ann was afraid to go → Ann was afraid to do it

Is that home baked? → Is that hard to bake?

room 260 is locked → is a lot

an errand to run near High Street → to run on new High Street

I don't think of the bass as a solo instrument → as so low an instrument

I need air → I need earmuffs

I don't think we could afford to bring him here → could get a Ford to bring him here

---

their perceptions and usually reported an utterance which contained the required function words. It is not possible to separate purely perceptual processes from the effects of memory or from a tendency to report the error as more grammatical than it was.

4.2.5. A Word Is Lost

There were several examples in which a word present in the target utterance was not perceived. In only two cases were content words clearly not perceived:

> an apartment for a hundred and ten a month → for ten a month
> The meaning of the word average has changed over the years
> → the mean of the average.

In the two other content word examples in Table 4.6, the content words are letter names given in spelling a word. In the remaining examples, the words which were not perceived were function words, hence unstressed and weakly articulated.

Some examples of word loss may result from editing, that is, ensuring that the utterance is grammatical. For example, the error

> change for a dollar → exchange a dollar

TABLE 4.6   Lost Element Is a Word

<u>Content word</u>

an apartment for a hundred and ten a month → for ten a month

The meaning of the word average has changed over the years → the mean of the average

P E O → B O

Clara W I E C K → W I Z K

<u>Function word</u>

Try newspaper and a hot iron → hot air

She wants to be a teacher → she wants me to teach her

change for a dollar → exchange a dollar

You're not wearing one → not married

It will be how many years? → It will be twenty years

Sara Garnes and Ilse → Sara Garnes Nielsen

I don't intend to stay in the picture → to stain the picture

Father Joe and → Father Joan

on an island with a moat surrounding it → with moats surrounding it

I know what happened to our ice, Andy → to high Sandy

cinema and photography → cinnamon photography

living with a coach → women who coach

---

would be the ungrammatical *exchange for a dollar* if the preposition had been retained perceptually. Not all reported errors were grammatical, however.

4.3. WORD BOUNDARIES

In the simplest cases of word boundary errors, all properties of the target utterance matched the perceived utterance except for the presence of word boundaries. In other words, the segments of the target utterance were almost identical to the perceived segments but word boundaries were misassigned. A classic error of this type is

> They had a ten-year party → a tenure party.

It is interesting to note that in all cases of word boundary loss, the environment for the loss is a stressed syllable followed by an unstressed syllable, a finding that supports Cutler's (1988) hypothesis that word boundaries tend to precede stressed syllables. The implications of word boundary additions and shifts are less clear. Although sometimes a word boundary is added preceding stressed syllables, as in

urination → you're a nation,

at other times, a word boundary addition or shift is not clearly related to the stress pattern of the target utterance. For example, in the misperception

Yoshimura → Yo Shimura,

the listener interpreted the Japanese surname as a given name plus surname but ignored alternating accent.

All examples of simple word boundary errors are given in Table 4.7.

In other cases, word boundary additions, losses, and shifts were accompanied by other errors. Word boundary additions are given in Table 4.8. It is possible to think of them as of two types. In the first type, the phonological material of the utterance remained roughly equivalent and a word boundary was added creating two content words. In the second type, the phonological material was reanalyzed to include a function word. The first type of error was considerably less common than the second type. Within the second type, the most common misperception involved an article, either added or formed from reanalysis of the a portion of the target.

Examples of word boundary loss are given in Table 4.9. These are classified whether the lost item seems to be a function word or whether the phonetic material is misanalyzed without a function word being lost. If the word boundary error involves more than one function word, the error is classified quite arbitrarily under the first function word affected.

There were fewer examples of a shift in word boundary, the number of word boundaries in the target and misperceived utterance remaining constant (see Table 4.10). A number of these involved misassigning a consonant, from word-initial to word-final position or the reverse, typically with other changes. For example,

Noel Matkin → Noam Atkin
this Acoustical Society → the Sacoustical Society.

4.4. MISORDERING

Sometimes misperceptions resulted in a change in the order of segments or syllables. This type of error also suggests that perception is not a matter of recovering a linear arrangement of segments but rather depends on a more global recovery of a target utterance. Misordering affected adjacent segments within a syllable in only one example:

TABLE 4.7   Simple Word Boundary Errors

Word boundary is lost

They had a ten-year party → a tenure party

lawn chair → launcher

We're going to pour him into the car → purim into the car

It costs six to seven dollars to replace → sixty-seven dollars

Mom, he did it → Mommy did it

He works in an herb and spice shop → an urban spice shop

four to five weeks → forty-five weeks

to go for Mike → Nicole for Mike

Chris De Pino → Christofino

SAS programing secrets → essayist programing secrets

Word boundary is added

"precise-ities" → precise cities

at the parasession → at the Paris session

Americana → a Mary Canna

Orrin W. Robinson → R. N. W. Robinson

everything's about a quarter more → about a quart or more

attacks in the ear → a tax on the ear

Yoshimura → Yo Shimura

acuteness feature → a cuteness feature

Word boundary is shifted

Do you know anything about four-term analogy? → about four terminology

We could give them an ice bucket → a nice bucket

this Acoustical Society → the Sacoustical Society

I scream → ice cream

good old zebra's law → zebra slaw

I need a loose crew → loose screw

notary public → Nota Republic

a bee flying backwards → a beef lying backwards

Dix Ward → Dick Sward

Polly played with Tom → polyp laden /θam/

Kate O'Berin → Kato Berin

TABLE 4.8   Word Boundaries Are Added

Word boundary

barbell set → bord la sell

myo-functional therapy → mild functional therapy

the paramour → the power mower

overcorrection → overt correction

back window → tack one doe

He runs a driving school → a drive-in school

I think it's a penguin → a pink one

Louisiana → New Zealand

osill → ass hole

She's working for the Judiciary Committee → for the Jewish charity committee

erudite → area dried

no bullshit exams → noble shit exams

meaningfulness → mean influence

a linguini is a noodle → a lean Wheatie is a noodle

meteor → meat eater

Added function word

Pronoun

She wants to be a teacher → she wants me to teach her

I love you and my baby → I love you. You are my baby.

Ann was afraid to go → afraid to do it

structure, style, and usage → instruct your style and usage

quiet → buy it

I lighted → I like it

Verbal element

This friend of ours who visited → of ours is an idiot

Anne Schwarz → had on shorts

hypnotic age regression → hypnotic aid to regression

Is that home baked? → Is that hard to bake?

I don't think we could afford to bring him here → could get a Ford to bring him here

Conjunction

It's a dollar a quarter → It's a dollar and a quarter

Jefferson Starship → Jeffers and starship

Skippers' treat → trick or treat

casual informal → casual and formal

(*Continues*)

TABLE 4.8   (*Continued*)

Preposition

You swallowed a watermelon → You smiled at a watermelon

That's the kind he used before → used in the Air Force

an errand to run near High Street → to run on New High Street

Someone else isn't neat this morning → is in heat this morning

They must be members of the Republican party → of the Republic of Hardy

parachute → pair of shoes

Sonic, the hedgehog → son of the hedgehog

Article

Room 260 is locked → is a lot

I don't think of the bass as a solo instrument → as so low an instrument

assorted → a sordid

Haggai's thesis → the guy's thesis

He's Snoopy in disguise → in the skies

Is he nasty? → Is he an ass?

Maybe we ought to give up descriptive linguistics → give up the script of linguistics

I'm not American → not a miracle

attorney Larry L. Rowe → a dirty Larry L. Rowe

I've been doing research → a search

> They're all Appalachian whites → Appalachian waste.

In this example, the /ts/ sequence of *whites* was reordered to a /st/ sequence. This is traditional metathesis.

More common were misordering of nonadjacent segments within a syllable, as in the following examples:

> Falstaff → Flagstaff
> Do you know a Greg Cortina → Do you own a Greg Cortina
> I can ink it in → can nick it in.

In these examples, as well as others of the same kind, the position of a segment within a syllable changed from initial to final. In the last example, the point of articulation of /ɔ/ was adjusted to /n/, as required by English phonotactics. In the example

> we offered six → we Alfred six,

a rhotacized vowel /ɝ/ was perceived as a sequence of /r/ followed by a vowel, suggesting that consonantal and vocalic /r/ share phonetic representations.

TABLE 4.9   Word Boundaries Are Lost

<u>Word boundary</u>

without your mother along → without your mother-in-law

Dec writer → decorator

your nation → urination

Well, I'll sit here and peck away some more → decolate some more

't shows → Joe's

I found it → Icelandic

Couldn't you say that was an SPC? → was misperceived?

low visibility → lovas

roll up the back window → patrol the back window

It'll be a confusing weekend → You're confusing weekends

You're not wearing one → not married

I didn't have to wear a coat → to work

No shit, Little Beaver → no shittling beaver

Mar Dee Doll → Marty Dow

I feel secure → I disappear

I'll catch my breath here → catch my breakfast

I'm covered with chalk dust → with chocolate

Anyone who thinks carob bean is a good substitute for chocolate is crazy → paraffin is a good
    substitute

First stop of his four nation tour → phonation tour

get my other cookbooks → my etiquette books

converge en masse → conversion mass

Get a pill out → a pillow

Mad River Township → Madrigal Township

I tripped on a tent pole → tadpole

I have them do out-of-class writing → auto class writing

We were in Amherst together → enamorous together

what Phil Morse is going to do → what Fillmore is going to do

I just like it → I dislike it

Herbert H. Lehman College → Heritage Lehman College

Geez, really? → Disraeli

catch a five-pounder → catch a flounder

That's a good way to get your car door taken off → your carburetor taken off

got a reaction → gonorrhea action

(Continues)

TABLE 4.9   *(Continued)*

I was running around after a slide projector → after a sniper

You've got all the books you need for the time being → for your typing

your nation → urination

no she isn't → no shitting

eat a Maple Leaf wiener → a make-believe wiener

This goes through forty-eight → through Fourier

He got ten years in prison → tenure in prison

I need to talk to him → I need to calculate

Thai food → typhoon

Function word

Prepositions

I don't intend to stay in the picture → to stain the picture

change for a dollar → exchange a dollar

We eat at eight → we needed eight

the floor of the house → the Florida house

in different positions → indifferent physicians

one cup of weak coffee → one Cocoa Wheat Puff

Verbal elements

I have to eat too → I have eighty-two

setting up of time → studying of time

I get to leave this place → I can't believe this place

with less than two weeks to go → less than two weeks ago

to go for Mike → Nicole for Mike

Conjunctions

Father Joe and . . . → Father Joan

Jean and I → Gina [unclear last name]

Legg and Davis → Leggett Davis

a purse and a billfold → a personal billfold

Coke and a Danish → coconut Danish

fruits and vegetables → prudent vegetables

Sara Garnes and Ilse → Sara Garnes Nielsen

cinema and photography → cinnamon photography

nose and eyes → Molson Ice

and tell → until

(Continues)

TABLE 4.9   *(Continued)*

Articles

Wouldn't she look good with a ring in her nose → oregano nose

I kept an eye on the Big Dipper last night → I kept denying the Big Dipper

he's out supervising the back hoe → supervising tobacco

on an island with a moat surrounding it → with moats surrounding it

A friend of ours is having a lung removed → is having alumni move

It's called *The Absence of a Cello* → *The Absence of Othello*

He was in a wreck → Iraq

Other

It will be how many years? → it will be twenty years

It's always too short → always toujours

I know what happened to our ice, Andy → to high Sandy

We had this appointment . . . → disappointment

TABLE 4.10   **Word Boundary Is Shifted**

Do you know *New Dimensions* → know nude mentions

I'm going up for my office hours → for my vodka sours

Noel Matkin → Noam Atkin

front vowels occur only in words → front vowels are Kyrolean words

your etiquette books → other cookbooks

I got to sleep at a decent hour → to sleep at least an hour

There's some ice tea made → there's a nice team mate

AHA → AAJ

We are not using the accident rates yet → not using the accident rate shit

this Acoustical Society → the Sacoustical Society

Hi-C → ice tea

we had a representative of the preschool come → of the Peace Corps

choose any nineteen → two seventy nineteen

kills germs where they grow → kills germs with egg roll

Ed McMahon → ethnic man

something like *Poseidon Adventure* → like a silent adventure

Do you have any aspirin? → have a napkin

Errors which involve misordering within a syllable do not have any analogue in production errors, that is, in slips of the tongue. In production errors, the position of a segment within a syllable appears to be resistant to modification whereas misperceived segments are not constrained by syllable position. Misorderings tended to be confined within syllables, however.

Examples of misorderings are given in Table 4.11.

4.5. GENERAL PROPERTIES OF MISPERCEPTIONS OF THE SHAPES OF WORDS

The diversity of theproperties that can be lost or changed in perception is impressive. There does not appear to be any one property of words which is invariably perceived correctly. The stress pattern may be misperceived, though relatively rarely. Syllables may be added or lost. In the vast majority of cases, these are unstressed, hence indistinct, syllables. Final syllables are affected much more frequently than initial or medial syllables. The addition and loss of syllables may result in a perceived word not being present in the target utterance or a word being lost. Typically affected are unstressed function words rather than stressed content words. Word boundaries can be added, lost, or shifted. Segments can be misordered, typically within syllables, rarely across syllable or word boundaries. Zwicky (1982) has compared slips of the ear with other types of performance errors. He finds that the error types are similar but their proportions differ.

We must conclude that no one property of words is safe from misperception. However, the distribution of errors suggests that some properties are more reliable than others. If any one were to be named as providing islands of relative reliability, it would be strong or stressed syllables.

TABLE 4.11　Misorderings

<u>Misorderings within a syllable</u>

They're all Appalachian whites → Appalachian waste

Bruce Galtter → Bruce Bladder

barbell set → bord la sell

speech science → speech sinus

Dennison → dentist

lunch in a huge cafeteria → in a Jewish cafeteria

Do you know a Greg Cortina → Do you own a Greg Cortina

Garnes → Garmens

Falstaff → Flagstaff

get your ducks in a row → get your guts in a row

movement → Newton

from 180 some → for 180 some

Is that margarine? → Is that Mondrian?

we offered six → we Alfred six

boustrophed[on]ic → Posturepedic

Siever's law → zebra's law

I have to eat too → I have eighty-two

Jane Kollaritsch → Jane Clark

I'm on a trip now → a chip one

We must get some sealing tape → ceiling paint

I can ink it in → can nick it in

How do you spell *Cochran* → spell *popcorn*

meaningfulness → mean influence

Mary, would you like some tea with this? → to eat with us

Do lions have manes? → have names

Think about your valves → your vowels

<u>Misorderings across a syllable boundary</u>

Acton Road → Atkin Road

without your mother along → without your mother-in-law

frothing → throfing

Janet Jackson → Chada Jackson

(Continues)

TABLE 4.11   (*Continued*)

Misorderings across a word boundary

found a copy → pound of coffee

spun toffee → fun stocking

I'm making boats → taking notes

she wants to be a teacher → she wants me to teach her

roll up the back window → patrol the back window

my three-ninety class → my three-D night class

CHAPTER 5

Children's Misperceptions

Children . . . seem to have mental representations of words
which are in a number of ways similar to those of adults. . .
                                    —Jean Aitchison (1987)

In our data, the number of children's misperceptions was small. One reason for this is the selection of conversational partners. Most adults spend more time talking with other adults than with children. Another reason for few child slips is that children tend not to report errors or to ask for clarification. For children, hearing incomprehensible adult speech is probably a fairly typical occurrence.

Although the data did not introduce any new processes not found in the patterns of misperceptions of adults, the overall impression created by the children's errors was that they used the knowledge of their language less and consequently were less constrained by linguistic knowledge than adults were. Alternatively, it may be that children indicate that they have experienced a slip of the ear only under very special circumstances.

5.1. VOWEL MISPERCEPTIONS

All examples of simple vowel errors are given in Table 5.1. All but three of these had stressed syllables as the targets. Front vowel targets were more common

TABLE 5.1   Simple Vowel Misperceptions

Syllable does not receive primary stress

enchilada → anchilada

I believe in Malcolm → in malko

That's a good local program → loco program

Tense–lax errors

We'll pick you up Saturday → will pick you up

a little pillbox → peel box

Vowel height errors

They have s's up there → asses

You are supposed to put *a* or *an* before the words → n /ɛn/

How do you spell *since*? → spell *sense*

Front–back errors

It's the Robin Hood principle → Rabin (/æ/) Hood

cuff him → cough him

Got milk? → gut milk

than central and back vowel targets. There were no misperceived diphthongs. A syllabic consonant was the target for two of the three misperceptions of secondary or unstressed syllables.

Children's misperceptions of stressed vowel targets did not differ appreciably from adult patterns. There were two errors affecting the tense—lax dimension: one of these involved a tense vowel being perceived as a lax vowel in a contraction; the other involved the reverse error, suggesting that children's perceptual errors followed the same pattern as did adult errors. In both, the affected vowels preceded /l/, an environment which obscures vowel quality.

Since the vowel height misperceptions showed errors in both directions, it seems reasonable to assume that both are likely for children just as they are for adults. In three of the words, the misperceived vowel occurred before a nasal consonant, so the influence of phonetic factors may be considerable. Just as for adults, the number of children's misperceptions in the front–back dimension was low.

Vowel errors as components of complex misperceptions are given in Table 5.2. In six of these errors an unstressed syllable was affected, and two of these were in function words. The remaining errors affected stressed sylla-

Table 5.2   Complex Vowel Errors

Unstressed syllable

initial → official

Your eyes are kind of bloodshot → kind of blushing

Feel this—it's cool → feel this at school

Mayor McCheese → Mayor get cheese

Iowa's colors → iris colors

We'll have to coordinate → have a quarter to eight

Vowel height errors

general → janitor

I'm feeling more cheery → more scary

What kind of accent do you think that was? → What kind of exit

the early administrations → menstrations

Isn't it nice not to have all these deadlines → all these dandelions

Don't mix up the code of the road → Don't make zip the code of the road

If you enjoyed Viet Nam → enjoyed meat an' ham

Front–back errors

ketchup → a chip

He pretended he didn't know what a pair of skis were → where a pair of skis were

book dump → mik dump

Biting dogs and crowing hens → curling hens

three-handed gin → three hundred gin

cigarettes → skrits

a rail to hang our lap robes on → our life robes on

one of us will be very sorry → very sour

bles. Front–back and vowel height errors occurred with approximately equal frequency.

5.2. CONSONANT MISPERCEPTIONS

Children's consonant misperceptions exhibited the same basic categories as adult misperceptions. However, the proportions with which certain errors occurred appeared to be different. In particular, there were few examples of consonant loss or addition but many of consonant substitution.

5.2.1. CONSONANT LOSS

There are only two examples of perceptual loss of target consonants:

> obstetrician → obsetrician
> The acts of God → The ax of God.

In the first example, a child heard a word of a rather complex phonological shape and repeated it, implicitly asking the adult speaker to tell him what the word means. It is possible that the child simply did not take in all segments of the target word on first hearing. It is also possible that the child heard the target word correctly but could not manage to repeat its complex phonological structure. In the second token, a child probably did not compensate for a simplified final consonant cluster, a phenomenon also noted in adult deletion errors.

Consonant loss as part of complex errors was much more frequent. Examples are given in Table 5.3. In only one of these was the consonant lost in initial position, and there were only three examples of consonant loss in medial position. By far the most common consonant loss was in final position, just as in the adult data.

5.2.2. CONSONANT ADDITIONS

There were more simple consonant addition errors for children than deletion errors, but the number was still quite small. All the children's addition errors were context free, none seemingly explicable in terms of the phonological structure of the target words.

Five of the children's additions were word-initial errors, and two were additions of the consonant /h/:

> usher → husher
> her obituary → her habituary.

Two other errors involved adding a word-initial voiced stop:

> this root → this brute
> There are some signs of an old mine → a gold mine.

One of the children's errors complicated a word-initial consonant cluster:

> Did you see the horse? It was spotted all over → splotted all over

The remaining consonant addition errors were medial:

> shivaree → chivalry
> fifty-six G's → jeans.

TABLE 5.3 Consonant Loss in Complex Errors

Initial position

ketchup → a chip

Medial position

I visited two classes today → missed two classes

the early administrations → menstrations

Final position

wax → glass

What the song "Half-breed" is all about → the song "Half-free"

Are you from Holland? → from pollen

What kind is it? → What time is it?

What kind of accent do you think that was? → what kind of exit

a matter of trial and error → trial and air

Your eyes are kind of blood shot → kind of blushing

I told him to go and find the store → infine the store

We'll have to coordinate → have a quarter to eight

She has green eyes → three eyes

Part of word loss

Where are your jeans? → Wear your jeans

Grandfather had a new lap robe → new Afro

How many miles is Hawaii from the mainland → from Dominion

There are stars and . . . → Tarzan

Though the number of tokens was small, there was some suggestion that children tend to make consonant addition errors in words which are rather unusual or novel. Certainly, most of the target words are unlikely to be part of a child's vocabulary.

Consonant additions as part of complex errors are given in Table 5.4. There were no clear positional preferences for addition errors—initial, medial, and final errors being approximately equally likely. The two errors

> I'm going to Miami → my yami
> The men are out lumbering in the forests → are out tlumbering

probably had the same source, a misassignment of word boundaries in which one consonant was assigned to two word positions. The second error is unique

TABLE 5.4   Consonant Additions as Part of Complex Errors

Initial position

I'm going to Miami → my yami

wax → glass

I'm feeling more cheery → more scary

The men are out lumbering in the forests → are out tlumbering

Medial position

Mayor McCheese → American cheese

three-handed gin → three hundred gin

Isn't it nice not to have all these deadlines → all these dandelions

We'll have to coordinate → have a quarter to eight

Final position

some bingo markers → bingle markers

if you enjoyed Vietnam → enjoyed meat an' ham

in that it is the only misperception which clearly violates English phonotactic constraints.

None of these errors appear to be related to inappropriate compensation for English phonological reduction rules, a source of consonant additions fairly common in the adult data.

5.2.3. CONSONANT SUBSTITUTIONS

The majority of children's manner substitutions occurred in word-initial position. Of the 12 manner errors for children in the data, 11 occurred word-initially while the remaining error was medial. As for adults, the majority of children's errors affected obstruents. Children's errors in the perception of manner are given in Table 5.5. In our data, three stops were perceived as fricatives and four fricatives were perceived as stops—a symmetry also found for adults. In the medial error, a lateral was perceived as a fricative:

molie → movie.

The patterns seem to be very similar to those of adults. Errors tended to be made between segments which are phonetically similar.

TABLE 5.5   Manner Substitution Errors

Initial position

home of the most famous ships that ply the seas → that fly the seas

Kon → Hon

They're getting off their course, you know → off their horse

Mrs. High → Mrs. Pie

she landed in a hole → pole

hold → cold

What's a CV? → CB

chip in a dollar → hip in

bury → marry

vampire → rampire

Letty Cooper → Betty Cooper

She has green eyes → three eyes

Medial position

molie → movie

Place errors were also quite common for children. Most errors were initial; medial and final errors occurred approximately half as often. The positional preferences of these children's errors were again very similar to adult errors. There were proportionately even fewer errors for resonant targets.

Of the errors in initial position, almost all targets were obstruents, primarily stops and fricatives. Since the misperceptions were all of low frequency, only one or two tokens of each type, no obvious generalizations are possible. In medial position, all the targets of misperception were stops. In final position, all but one of the error targets were stops. These data are given in Table 5.6.

Even though the total corpus of misperceptions for children was considerably smaller than for adults, there were more voicing errors attested for children, not just proportionately but in absolute numbers. Half of the errors involved perceiving a voiced consonant as voiceless; the other half involved the reverse error. The medial error

pedal to the metal → to the medal

was probably very similar to the adult error in which a flap was misanalyzed as a voiced rather than a voiceless stop. Examples of voicing errors are given in Table 5.7.

TABLE 5.6   Place of Articulation Substitutions

Initial position

The FDIC is here on the right → FBIC

Well, how about a plosive? → a klosive

Family Plot → Family Klott

Look at this dirt → this girt

that's a phi → a thigh

I'm not going to Dayton tomorrow → Payton tomorrow

Medial position

I wonder if they thought the windows were thermopanes → thermotanes

Mr. Hawbecker → Mr. Hawdecker

Do you know what *taksi* means in Finnish? → what *tapsy* means in Finnish

The Big Leaguer → The Big Leader

That's ungrammatical speech → undramatical speech

Final position

They held a sheet up in front of the married couple → held a sheep

Let's look for the cape → the cake

That's no trick → no trip

Do you want a coat? → a Coke

Would you get the coats? → Cokes

chine tool → chime tool

comics → comets

corset → corsep

Examples of consonant substitutions as part of complex errors are given in Table 5.8. The most common targets for misperceptions were obstruents, with nasals, liquids, and glides providing fewer targets. There may be a tendency for some substitution errors to be related to word boundaries in that a consonant or some property of a consonant spread from one word to a following word. At least that is a possible interpretation of errors such as

> *Poor Richard's Almanac* is full of homey advice → phony advice
> I was looking at this photograph → this soda graph.

In the misperception

> cigarettes → skrits

TABLE 5.7   Errors in Voicing

Initial position

vase → face

Je ne sais pas → *Je ne sais ba* [English speakers]

I got it at the Tall shop → doll shop

Medial position

Do you have a nibble? → Do you have a nipple?

I put it in my book bag → in my book back

How do you spell *savor?* → spell *safer*

Final position

I think they're going to do the warts first → the wards

pedal to the metal → to the medal

English phonotactics were influencing the misperception in that the voiced stop is perceived as voiceless when missing a vowel makes it part of a cluster.

5.3. ERRORS IN THE PERCEPTION OF THE SHAPE OF WORDS

5.3.1. WORD BOUNDARY ERRORS

Children made word boundary errors at a slightly higher rate than adults did, though the patterns were otherwise quite similar. In our data, loss, insertion, and deletion of word boundaries appeared to be equally likely. The examples of word boundary errors with minimal segmental changes are given in Table 5.9. In one example,

triangular → try angular,

a word boundary is inserted before a stressed syllable. In two examples a word boundary is lost, in both cases creating words beginning with unstressed syllables. Cutler and Norris (1988) describe adult strategies for segmenting continuous speech which involve placing word boundaries before stressed syllables. These data suggest that at least some children may still be in the process of developing adult strategies for segmenting continuous speech.

TABLE 5.8   Consonant Substitutions as Part of Complex Errors

Obstruents

He pretended he didn't know what a pair of skis were → where a pair of skis were

the warts first → wards first

book dump → mik dump

a rail to hang our lap robes on → our life robes on

what the song "Half-breed" is all about → the song "Half-free"

Are you from Holland? → from pollen

What kind is it? → What time is it?

Poor Richard's Almanac is full of homey advice → phony advice

I visited two classes today → missed two classes

Grandfather had a new lap robe → new Afro

Your eyes are kind of bloodshot → kind of blushing

they are on late → on a lake

Don't mix up the code of the road → Don't make zip the code of the road

I was looking at this photograph → this soda graph

cigarettes → skrits

How many miles is Hawaii from the mainland? → from Dominion

Nasals

initial → official

Mayor McCheese → Mayor get cheese

Where did you get your tallness from? → your tongs from

If you enjoyed Vietnam → enjoyed meat an' ham

Liquids and glides

general → janitor

wax → glass

Iowa's colors → iris colors

Biting dogs and crowing hens → curling hens

Mayor McCheese → American cheese

TABLE 5.9   Word Boundary Errors with Minimal Associated Segmental Errors

to missions → temissions

Feel this—it's cool → feel this at school

triangular → try angular

Would you like to be a maid? → be amayd

Curiously two of the errors resulted in nonwords. Chaney (1989) suggests that children tend to convert more abstract and unfamiliar words into simpler vocabulary when asked to segment well-known passages. There is some support for this strategy provided by examples such as

If you enjoyed Vietnam → enjoyed meat an' ham
We'll have to coordinate → have a quarter to eight

in which words that are probably unfamiliar to children are replaced by more familiar terms. Counter to this tendency, however, is the tendency to report nonwords.

The remaining errors in word boundary assignment are given in Table 5.10. These errors also result in quite a few nonwords.

The examples of inserted and shifted word boundaries suggest that children are following adult strategies. The implications from examples of lost word boundaries are less clear.

TABLE 5.10   Misperceptions of Word Boundaries in Combination with Other Errors

Lost

Grandfather had a new lap robe → Afro

I told him to go and find the store → infine the store

How many miles is Hawaii from the mainland? → from Dominion

There are stars and . . . → Tarzan

Where are your jeans? → Wear your jeans

Your eyes are kind of bloodshot → kind of blushing

Inserted

Mayor McCheese → Mayor get cheese

I'm going to Miami → my yami

If you enjoyed Vietnam → enjoyed meat an' ham

We'll have to coordinate → have a quarter to eight

Shifted

Mayor McCheese → American cheese

Don't mix up the code of the road → Don't make zip the code of the road

The men are out lumbering in the forests → are out tlumbering

5.3.2. Ordering Errors

In the children's data, there was only one example which appears to involve mis-ordering of segments:

> lots of laminated wood → animated wood.

In the misperception, the order of two syllable-initial nasal consonants was reversed. Even when the smaller sample of children's errors is considered, the minimal number of ordering errors was rather surprising in that, according to the folklore of child language, ordering errors such as *cimanom* for *cinnamon* and *pasghetti* for *spaghetti* are common.

5.3.3. Change in Syllable Number

Of the examples of misperceptions in the number of syllables, there were only two instances of perceiving extraneous syllables; though the match between the target utterances and the misperceptions was far from clear, both apparently involved adding unstressed syllables. The remaining examples of change in syllable number involved loss of a syllable, in all cases unstressed (see Table 5.11).

TABLE 5.11   Change in Syllable Number

Syllable is added

Mayor McCheese → American cheese

Isn't it nice not to have all these deadlines → all these dandelions

Syllable is lost

Iowa's colors → iris colors

one of us will be very sorry → very sour

I visited two classes today → missed two classes

Asbjorn Olafson Vinje → Asjorn Olaf Vinje

cigarettes → skrits

We're going on the Horace Mann Run → horse man run

Where did you get your tallness from? → your tongs from

a matter of trial and error → trial and air

the early administrations → menstrations

Where are your jeans? → Wear your jeans

In four examples, one or both of the syllables ended in /r/, apparently an environment which makes syllable loss somewhat more likely. The error

Where are your jeans? → Wear your jeans

involves loss of the word *are,* which may have been contracted in the target utterance. The lost syllable turns a question into a command.

5.3.4. SHIFT IN STRESS PATTERN

Changes in the stress pattern were extremely infrequent in the child data. There were only two examples:

Mayor McCheese → American cheese
ketchup → a chip

Since these were associated with word boundary errors, it is not possible to say whether the children were using a strategy of looking for the most typical stress pattern for words from syntactic classes.

5.4. CHILDREN'S LEXICON

The most prominent characteristic of the children's lexicon was the perception of nonwords. Other errors involving morphology in one way or another were few.

5.4.1. NONWORDS

Children made proportionally more errors resulting in non-English words than adults did, perhaps because of the youngsters' relatively limited lexicon. With the exception of *tlumbering,* all the nonwords were phonologically well formed. Five resulted from word boundary misassignment, and two from syllable loss. The remaining two nonwords involved fairly straightforward segmental substitutions. These data are given in Table 5.12.

5.4.2. INFLECTION, DERIVATION, AND CLITICS

Because the misperceptions recorded for children were often short and fragmentary, there were few examples of errors which involved morphology. The

TABLE 5.12   Perceived Nonwords

It's the Robin Hood principle → Rabin (/æ/) Hood
enchilada → anchilada
I'm going to Miami → my yami
book dump → mik dump
Are you from Holland? → from pollen
the early administrations → menstrations
to missions → temissions
I told him to go and find the store → infine the store
The men are out lumbering in the forests → are out tlumbering
cigarettes → skrits
Would you like to be a maid? → be amayd

errors seem to be reinterpretations of existing phonetic information. In one error, a word with a plural affix was interpreted as monomorphemic:

Iowa's colors → iris colors.

In another error, a derivational affix was reinterpreted as a plural:

Where did you get your tallness from? → your tongs from?

Both of these errors seem to be motivated by phonological information rather than by morphological processes in that both misperceptions have phonetic support. The same can be said for the error in which a syllable of a monomorphemic word was interpreted as an affix:

How do you spell *savor*? → spell *safer*?

Three errors affected contracted forms. In the first, a pronoun contracted with a modal lost the pronoun:

We'll pick you up Saturday → will pick you up.

Another contraction was interpreted as a preposition

Feel this—it's cool → feel this at school.

As mentioned above, a misinterpreted contraction lead to recasting a sentence from a question to an imperative:

Where are your jeans? → Wear your jeans.

5.4.3. FUNCTION WORDS

Children interpreted unstressed syllables as function words and treated function words as parts of lexical items. All examples involved other phonological readjustments. Although the total number of errors was small, three involved the conjunction *and*:

> If you enjoyed Vietnam → enjoyed meat an' ham
> I told him to go and find the store → infine the store
> There are stars and . . . → Tarzan.

In another misperception of function words, the infinitive marker *to* was reinterpreted as a preposition:

> We'll have to coordinate → have a quarter to eight.

As in adult errors, function words could be added as required by grammatical considerations:

> They are on late → on a lake.

Children also appear to edit perceptions.

5.5. SYNTAX

A number ofchildren's misperceptions lead to unlikely or ungrammatical phrases or sentences. In the slip

> cuff him → cough him,

the misperceived vowel leads to a verb which is not commonly transitive. The misperception

> Don't mix up the code of the road → Don't make zip the code of the road

seems ungrammatical. The slip

> Got milk? → gut milk,

a misinterpretation of a television commercial, is grammatical but not particularly meaningful or interpretable. The same could be said for the slip

> Mayor McCheese → Mayor get cheese.

Syntactic structure does not seem to impose many constraints on the interpretation of phrases and sentences.

5.6. GENERAL TENDENCIES

Most of the characteristics of perceptual errors of children and of adults seem to be very similar, suggesting that children's perceptual strategies are relatively similar to adult strategies. But there were some differences which can best be attributed to children's lack of linguistic knowledge.

Children appeared to be using less knowledge of English phonology and lexicon than adult listeners did. Children made few errors which depend on phonological knowledge, whereas adults reported perceived consonants expected from English phonology. The one child error violating phonotactic constraints also suggested that children are more flexible, that is, less restricted by knowledge of their language. Children made more errors which resulted in English nonwords, probably because they are still increasing their lexicon at a rapid rate and expect to hear new words. Children seem to be willing to report odd or ungrammatical sentences. Finally, children may still be developing strategies for segmenting continuous speech for lexical access.

CHAPTER 6

The Lexicon

How often do speakers . . . encounter new words?
—R. Harald Baayen (1994)

The perceptual errors in which the target and the misperception differ by a segment or two are much more transparent than errors which depart in extensive ways from their targets. These errors are often funny and bizarre; they are sometimes suggestive, providing information about the sources of knowledge that listeners have and the ways that they use knowledge when dealing with ordinary language. Although the implications are not always particularly clear, it is possible to make some observations about the structure of the lexicon and the role of various types of words in sentence understanding.

6.1. NONWORDS

One interesting characteristic of slips of the ear is that they on occasion result in the perception of nonwords. When listeners reported that they had heard nonwords, they often remarked on this as an odd or curious experience. The examples are given in Table 6.1.

There are probably multiple reasons for the perception of nonwords. In some circumstances, listeners may have had no expectations or insufficient

TABLE 6.1   Misperceptions Leading to Nonwords

Misperception of a vowel

Did I ever tell you about this usher? → this esher

You know that soil can be → swail can be

kings → kangs

It's a chain tool → chine tool

He's going to write a paper on tonology → on tenology

Misperception of a consonant

Skandinavian languages → Standinavian

The mining of Haiphong harbor → Haithong harbor

phone → thone

atmosphere → atnosphere

There's a word I learned in high school—*slovern* → *slobbern*

who? → oo

Wie geht's → i gates

the article → the yarticle

sitter problems → sinter

booty → boolie

Yosemite → Dosemite

He understands move → mooth

cushion sole → kutchion sole

slip of the ear, *tlumbering* → *klumbering*

Complex misperceptions

barbell set → bord la sell

low visibility → lovas

hero sandwich → harrah sandwich

go to a party → to a burly

a process of residence selection → residence lection

a fancy seductive letter → a fancy structive letter

No shit, Little Beaver → no shittling beaver

We're going to pour him into the car → purim into the car

back window → tack one doe

So you're going to be there two years in a row? → to be edder
two years

notary public → Nota republic

(Continues)

TABLE 6.1 *(Continued)*

frothing → throfing

Star Fire → /sta fa/

the anechoic chamber → the ambionic chamber

Paula played with Tom → polyp laden /θam/

avalanche → evelinsh

knowledge to guide them, as in the case of proper names. This may also be the case with a number of other misperceptions which involved specialized or unusual vocabulary such as *anechoic* or *tonology*. The context for *slovern* suggests that the speaker was not sure whether the listener was familiar with the word. The slip *evelinsh* for *avalanche* occurred in a conversation about the hockey player Ozolinsh, so may show perceptual contamination from discourse.

One target was a nonword, perceived as a phonologically well-formed nonword:

slip of the ear, *tlumbering* → *klumbering*

In the example

Wie geht's → i gates

the listener was probably not expecting to hear a German phrase. These perceptions of nonwords could have occurred when the listeners could not find a word in their lexicons.

Other nonwords resulted from failure to compensate for the dialect of the speakers. The listeners had accurate phonetic information but could not use it appropriately. The two examples are:

kings → kangs

Star Fire → /sta fa/

The first misperception probably resulted from the well-known difficulties with lax vowels before nasals. In the second example, the first speaker asked for the name of a gas station that could supply a tow truck. She was told to "Call Star Fire in the Plains" in an *r*-less dialect. Her perception was phonetically accurate, but the phonetic information did not match a known proper name in her lexicon and she had insufficient knowledge about the dialect of the first speaker to make the necessary adjustments.

Even though some misperceptions leading to nonwords may result from lack of knowledge or from relaxed expectations, the majority of nonword misperceptions must have other sources since common words were also misperceived, e.g., *sitter, party,* or *back window.*

TABLE 6.2   Perceived Nonwords

It's the Robin Hood principle → Rabin (/æ/) Hood

I'm going to Miami → my yami

book dump → mik dump

enchilada → anchilada

Are you from Holland? → from pollen

the early administrations → menstrations

to missions → temissions

I told him to go and find the store → infine the store

The men are out lumbering in the forests → are out tlumbering

cigarettes → skrits

Would you like to be a maid? → be amayd

The occasional report of nonexistent lexical items suggests that listeners must be able to develop a phonological representation of what they hear. Otherwise, there could be no source for the nonexistent words which listeners were willing to report. See Aitchison (1987) for an informative discussion concerning this topic.

Children made proportionately more errors which resulted in nonexistent words than adults did. Since children are probably adding words to their vocabulary at a rapid rate, they may expect to hear words with which they are not yet familiar. Children's misperceptions leading to nonexistent words are listed in Table 6.2, repeating data from Chapter 5.

There are many legendary examples of erroneous lexical representations from the speech of children. Apparently these arise when children are asked to learn by rote material which exceeds their comprehension. For example, from the Lord's Prayer, we have "halovanina" for "hallowed be thy name" also "Gladly, the cross-eyed bear" from the hymn "Gladly the Cross I'd Bear" (see Aitchison, 1972; Vihman, 1981). Adults are not immune to such errors either, as attested by a misinterpretation of a line from a Beatles song, "the girl with kaleidoscope eyes," as "the girl with colitis goes by."

It is possible that some mistaken lexical representations have originated as misperceptions which were stored in the mental lexicon. There were only a few examples, all reported by adults; in one of these, the target was a proper name:

> Levi Jackson → Levi Jetson
> bandwagon → ban wagon
> frothing → throfing
> for all intents and purposes → for all intensive purposes.

Zwicky's (1979) discussion of classical malapropisms includes examples which are related to slips of the ear. Examples of reanalysis or folk etymology, such as *duck tape* for *duct tape, windshield factor* for *windchill factor,* and *very close veins* for *varicose veins* are undoubtedly related as well.

6.2. WORD FREQUENCY

In almost all experimental investigations of word recognition, word frequency is a powerful factor. It is common for word recognition models to be devised to deal with word frequency effects and even to use word frequency in the strategies proposed for accessing the mental lexicon. Forster (1976), for example, argues that words are arranged by frequency in an access file.

The perception of nonwords is difficult to reconcile with word frequency effects in that a nonword by definition has no frequency of occurrence and should not be perceived at all. Nevertheless, the perception of nonwords may be special, brought about by unusual circumstances in a conversation.

There would be value in determining whether misperceptions are influenced by word frequency. It is certainly plausible that a listener faced with imprecise phonological information reports the more frequent word. The simplest prediction would be that more frequent words tend to replace rare words.

In order to test that prediction, the frequency of a sample of target words and their misperceptions were compared. A sample of adult misperceptions which were involved in relatively simple errors was selected at random. All words which include any proper names, even commonly used trade names such as Coke or Dec, were eliminated.

According to the Kučera and Francis (1967) word frequency counts, the results showed a virtual tie. In the 75 comparisons, a more frequent word replaced a rarer word 36 times; a rarer word replaced a more frequent word 39 times. Thus, the simple prediction was not supported.

These results do not refute the suggestion that word frequency operates in the perception of casual conversation. First, when listeners reported perceptual errors, they were undoubtedly more likely to notice unusual rather than common slips; that is, the data set may be biased to begin with. Second, word frequency may be a powerful factor when all things are equal, but examples in the error data are probably influenced by syntactic and pragmatic context and phonological structure, as well as other factors, in ways which are complex and not yet clear.

That word intelligibility is not significantly influenced by word frequency has been observed by Hood and Poole (1980). Pisoni, Luce, and Nusbaum (1986) have suggested that the phonetic similarity of targets to other words is an important moderator of word frequency effects.

6.3. MORPHOLOGY

6.3.1. INFLECTION AND DERIVATION

One of the debates about the mental lexicon concerns the access and under-standing of morphologically complex words. One view is that words are ac-cessed from their stems after affixes are removed. Alternatively, complex words may be stored as wholes in the lexicon in association with morphologically re-lated forms. Within the lexicon, morphology may be viewed as actively in-volved in language use or as passive knowledge. Inflectional and derivational morphemes may or may not function in the same way in the organization of the lexicon or in language use (see Marslen-Wilson, 1989). The organization of noun inflections is discussed by Feldman and Fowler (1987), Lukatela, Gligorijevic, Kostic, Savic, and Turvey (1978), and Lukatela, Gligorijevic, Kostic, and Turvey (1980).

The answers to these issues provided by the misperception data are ulti-mately ambiguous because the theories do not make clear predictions about the processes used in ordinary language understanding.

Monomorphemic words were reported as consisting of two morphemes but less frequently than the reverse error—hearing a word with an affix as a monomorphemic word. This pattern suggests that listeners favor monomor-phemic forms, an error type consistent with the idea that listeners strip affixes from stems, if we assume that finding an affix is an additional step.

Examples of the first type of error, interpreting monomorphemic words as words with affixes without extensive phonological restructuring, are given in Table 6.3. The most common error type was to report a plural form in place of a singular form. Most errors involved interpreting phonetic material as an affix rather than as part of the word, sometimes across a word boundary. That is, there was phonological support for the error. For example,

> dialect divergence → dialect diversions
> on an island with a moat surrounding it → with moats surrounding it.

Other misperceptions did not have obvious phonological support but probably appeared as a result of editing, that is, conforming the perception to grammatical requirements. For example,

> It'll be a confusing weekend → You're confusing weekends
> parachute → pair of shoes

The motivation for some examples is opaque, as in

> the most literate → most illiterate.

Reinterpreting the phonological material as consisting of a monomorphemic word rather than of a word with an affix was much more common. This find-

TABLE 6.3   One Morpheme Is Interpreted as Two

Inflection

Plural

the white sauce ladies → the white socks ladies

dialect divergence → dialect diversions

Her niece was in the hospital → her knees

It will be done next year → in six years

on an island with a moat surrounding it → with moats surrounding it

parachute → pair of shoes

Anne Schwarz → had on shorts

Other

This is six news at eight → Dick's news

It'll be a confusing weekend → You're confusing weekends

a loose end in this problem → a leaf's end

Does he have any hair? → any higher

I was through on a bus → I was thrown off a bus

Couldn't you say that was an SPC? → was misperceived

Derivation

He hasn't heard of any viable reasons → buyable reasons

How do you spell *diverse*? → *divert*

felicity conditions → ballistic conditions

the most literate → most illiterate

---

ing is consistent with the observation that listeners tend to report monomorphemic forms when they are presented with one vs. two morpheme homophones. For example, when presented with /blu/, listeners tend to write *blue* rather than *blew*. Those examples which do not show extensive phonologi- cal changes are given in Table 6.4.

Sometimes the phonological material was simply reinterpreted, as in the following examples:

matches → mattress
I lighted → I like it
good old zebra's law → zebra slaw.

Other examples of reinterpretation apparently had less obvious motivation. Most examples affected inflectional rather than derivational affixes. This may simply result from the fact that, in conversation, inflected forms are more common than derived forms.

TABLE 6.4   An Affix Is Reinterpreted as Part of a Stem

Plural

the acts of God → the ax of God

those shoes → oh, shoot

matches → mattress

book on primate infants → primate incest

It depends on the Finns → on the spin

They're all Appalachian whites → Appalachian waste

He got ten years in prison → tenure in prison

How about your tires? → your title

There are stars and . . . → Tarzan

Participles

Who's calling? → Who's Colleen?

plant dying → plant dung

He runs a driving school → a drive-in school

citrus craving → citrus gravy

interestin' → Enarson

cracked → track

my coffee cup refilled → my coffee cup fell

Posessives

I've never cooked anybody's goose → cooked anybody mousse

Olga's son → the sun

good old zebra's law → zebra slaw

Skippers' Treat → trick or treat

Joe's going to → jaws going to

Other

This friend of ours who visited → of ours is an idiot

R.P.ized → RPI

There were only three examples of an affix being reinterpreted as a different affix. All three examples were inflectional suffixes:

> Long's → lawns
> missed the news → must a snoozed
> 't shows → Joe's.

It is worth adding that various perceptual errors could take place in a stem without affecting affixes. For example,

> I read Coomb's paper last night → Kuhn's paper
> Bloomfield's personality was warped here → Whorfed here
> I have to say good-bye to the Frys → flies.

In the first example, a name was misperceived but its possessive suffix remained unaffected. In the second example, a past tense suffix was retained in the misperception even when the target was heard as a proper noun forming a nonce form. In the third example, the plural suffix was perceived correctly while the noun was perceived erroneously.

6.3.2. Contracted Forms

There are very few clear examples of errors in which clitics are involved. All are contracted forms. The relevant examples are given in Table 6.5.

Although there are only a few examples of such errors, the impression left by these slips is that contracted forms are no different from words with affixes.

As is the case with affixes, contracted forms were perceived correctly even when their hosts were not. For example,

> That's a good idea for the future → What's a good idea
> She doesn't know what he's doing? → know what she's doing
> Andy's going to fall asleep → Annie's
> There's Jay → Where's Jay?

TABLE 6.5   Errors Involving Clitics

<u>Contracted forms lost</u>

the bottom's all covered with eels → the bob . . .

it's typed → his type

In four to six months we'll get a house → four to six marks will get you a house

someone else isn't neat this morning → is in heat this morning

<u>Contracted forms created</u>

I get to leave this place → I can't believe this place

I can see you at four → I can't see you at four

Worse 'n that → Where's Annette

<u>Other</u>

I'm horny → It's morning

It'll be a confusing weekend → You're confusing weekends

6.4. FUNCTION WORDS

There has been speculation that function words provide information about the thematic roles of various constituents (see, e.g., Kimball, 1973). The misperception data do not provide an unambiguous answer about the role of function words, but there were many examples which suggest that the syntactic information provided by function words can be obliterated by other considerations. In a number of examples, a function word was misperceived as another function word with other errors minimally involved:

> That's a good idea for the future → What's a good idea
> When were you here? → Why were you here?
> It will be how many years? → It will be twenty years
> from 180 some → for 180 some
> those shoes → oh, shoot
> We'll pick you up Saturday → will pick you up
> I think I see a place → I think I see his face
> Did you put the food out for him? → for them
> Worse 'n that → Where's Annette
> this nation → the station.

In some of these, the misperceived word changed the function of an utterance from a declarative sentence to a question or from a question to an imperative phrase. There were also examples of a misperception leading to a negative reading of a positive sentence:

> Let me now try to develop this point → not try to develop
> I can see you at four → I can't see you at four.

Another example involved a change in the polarity of a sentence with other changes:

> someone else isn't neat this morning → is in heat this morning.

In one case, a misperceived function word was associated with a change of the verb *typed* into a noun:

> It's typed → his type.

One sequence of function words was reported as a meaningless lexical item, a nonword:

> So you're going to be there two years in a row? → to be edder two years.

These misperceptions of function words indicate that the syntactic structure of a sentence can be altered and that its new interpretation can arise from the misperceived function words as well as from other sources.

Those examples of function words in the target utterance which were misperceived with a concomitant word boundary error are given in Table 6.6. These data do not have one simple interpretation. In some cases, a misperceived function word apparently lead to a syntactic reading of an utterance which was completely congruent with the new function word. In other cases, function words were edited to report a grammatical sentence. In still other cases, the perceived sentences were ungrammatical or at least doubtful. Consequently, it is impossible to clarify the role of function words in providing cues to syntactic structure from the examples of perceptual errors. However, the data suggest that function words are not a primary source of information for determining syntactic structure.

One perceptual error involving a function word clearly happened "on line." The speaker began a sentence with

We had this appointment . . .

The listener interrupted the speaker, asking

disappointment

with a question intonation. The listener failed to detect a word boundary and interpreted the sequence beginning with a function word as a plausible lexical

TABLE 6.6   Function Word Targets and Word Boundary Errors

she wants to be a teacher → she wants me to teach her

This friend of ours who visited → of ours is an idiot

I love you and my baby → I love you. You are my baby.

change for a dollar → exchange a dollar

It'll be a confusing weekend → You're confusing weekends

I didn't have to wear a coat → to work

It will be how many years? → It will be twenty years

We were in Amherst together → enamorous together

Sara Garnes and Ilse → Sara Garnes Nielsen

got a reaction → gonorrhea action

You've got all the books you need for the time being → for your typing

your nation → urination

I don't intend to stay in the picture → to stain the picture

Father Joe and . . . → Father Joan

no, she isn't → no shitting

on an island with a moat surrounding it → with moats surrounding it

choose any nineteen → two seventy nineteen

I don't think of the bass as a solo instrument → as so low an instrument item. This interchange offers further support for the conclusion that function words are not invariable guides to syntactic structure.

6.5. SUBSTITUTIONS

Sometimes listeners seem to be quite inattentive to phonetic information and report a word only vaguely related to the speaker's utterance. What makes these substitutions curious is that the target and the misperception seem to come from the same semantic domain. There are only a few examples:

> Athens → Akron
> pathology → psychology
> sounds interesting → intriguing.

6.6. RELIABLE INFORMATION

6.6.1. STRESSED VOWELS

There is a strong belief held by many researchers that vowels or perhaps stressed vowels provide reliable information for lexical access. Grosjean and Gee (1987) argue that "stressed syllables (and only they) are used to initiate a lexical search. . . . [C]oncurrently, the weak syllables located on either side of the stressed syllable . . . are identified by means of a pattern-recognition-like analysis and with the help of the listener's knowledge of phonotactic and morphophonemic rules" (p. 144). Cutler and her colleagues (Cutler & Norris, 1988; Butterfield & Cutler, 1988; Cutler & Butterfield, 1992) propose that stressed syllables provide information for segmenting the continuous speech stream. Specifically, listeners tend to assume that strong or stressed syllables begin content words. Listeners tend to associate weak or unstressed syllables with preceding strong syllables or to treat them as function words.

There are two ways in which the perceptual errors can provide relevant data. First, errors in word boundary assignment should be associated with stressed vowels. Specifically, spurious word boundaries should tend to be inserted before stressed syllables and word boundaries should be lost in sequences of unstressed syllables. Second, word boundary errors might be associated with errors in stress patterns or with errors in the perception of stressed vowels.

6.6.1.1. Word Boundary Errors and Stress

Examples of word boundary loss without accompanying radical phonological restructuring indicated that there was a tendency to associate unstressed or weakly stressed syllables with a preceding stressed syllable. Apparently, listeners expect words to begin with stressed syllables and to contain a number of following unstressed syllables. Relevant examples are given in Table 6.7. In fact, there were only two potential counterexamples in which unstressed syllables were associated with following stressed syllables rather than preceding stressed syllables:

Do you know anything about four-term analogy? → about four terminology
He's out supervising the back hoe → supervising tobacco.

Apparently, listeners expect that words will consist of stressed syllables followed by unstressed syllables.

When spurious word boundaries were inserted, they were also sensitive to stress patterns. In most of the examples with little phonological restructuring, a long word was fragmented. The extraneous word boundary was typically placed before a syllable receiving stress. These data are given in Table 6.8.

However, there were a few examples which showed a countertendency. In these, an unstressed syllable became a separate lexical item.

Orrin W. Robinson → R. N. W. Robinson
everything's about a quarter more → about a quart or more

The first of these counterexamples is suspect in that it involves a proper name which is interpreted as two initials. Proper names may not provide information concerning general strategies used in lexical access.

Both addition and loss of word boundaries seem to be related to expected word stress patterns, judging by examples which do not involve massive restructuring of the phonological material.

TABLE 6.7 Word Boundaries Are Lost, Associating Unstressed Syllables with Preceding Stressed Syllable

they had a ten-year party → a tenure party

lawn chair → launcher

We're going to pour him into the car → purim into the car

it costs six to seven dollars to replace → sixty-seven dollars

without your mother along → without your mother-in-law

Mom, he did it → Mommy did it

Jean and I → Gina [unclear last name]

He works in an herb and spice shop → an urban spice shop

cinema and photography → cinnamon photography

four to five weeks → forty-five weeks

TABLE 6.8   Word Boundaries Are Added Preceding Stressed Syllables

urination → you're a nation
"precise-ities" → precise cities
at the parasession → at the Paris session
Americana → a Mary Canna
attacks in the ear → a tax on the ear
acuteness feature → a cuteness feature

6.6.1.2. Word Boundary and Stressed Vowel Errors

Since stressed syllables seem to be perceptually salient, we might expect word boundary misperceptions to be related to stressed vowel misperceptions. It turns out that the relationship between the two is not particularly illuminating. Word boundary errors associated with stressed vowel errors (without other radical phonetic errors) are given in Table 6.9. Though an overall phonetic resemblance characterized the errors, it is not obvious that there is any clear relationship between word boundaries and vowel errors beyond the observation that word boundaries seem to be lost more than added.

Word boundary errors associated with unstressed vowel errors are given in Table 6.10. Although the total number of errors was small, the majority of these were examples of word boundary loss. This finding supports the suggestion that unstressed syllables tend to be associated with stressed syllables in word boundary assignment.

Perhaps word boundary errors are associated with errors in the perception of stress patterns because listeners expect word boundaries to be related to stressed syllables. Those examples which show errors in both stress and word boundary assignment are given in Table 6.11. All these examples showed some phonological resemblance between the target and the misperception. However, word boundaries were added, deleted, or shifted in a pattern that did not have any clear relationship to stress. The errors have little to say about the very appealing idea that stressed syllables guide word boundary placement and therefore are relevant to lexical access.

6.6.2. SYLLABLE STRUCTURE

Kaye (1989), among others, has suggested that syllable structure might mediate between the acoustic signal and the phonological representations of words. Cutler, Mehler, Norris, and Segui (1989) have presented experimental data which suggest that the perceptual function of syllables is dependent on specific characteristics of languages. Speakers of languages such as French, with clearly

TABLE 6.9   Word Boundary and Stressed Vowel Errors

I found it → Icelandic

Couldn't you say that was an SPC? → was misperceived?

I love you and my baby → I love you. You are my baby.

Is that home baked? → Is that hard to bake?

I kept an eye on the Big Dipper last night → I kept denying the Big Dipper

I feel secure → I disappear

I get to leave this place → I can't believe this place

I just like it → I dislike it

Geez, really? → Disraeli

no, she isn't → no shitting

You swallowed a watermelon → You smiled at a watermelon

Ann was afraid to go → afraid to do it

I didn't have to wear a coat → to work

I feel secure → I disappear

It's always too short → always toujours

Anyone who thinks carob bean is a good substitute for chocolate is crazy → paraffin is a good substitute

get my other cookbooks → my etiquette books

your etiquette books → other cookbooks

I get to leave this place → I can't believe this place

Dec writer → decorator

no, she isn't → no shitting

we had a representative of the preschool come → of the Peace Corps

I'm not American → not a miracle

I think it's a penguin → a pink one

osill → ass hole

marked syllable boundaries, use syllables in perceptual segmentation. Speakers of languages such as English, with relatively unclear syllable boundaries, do not.

It is not entirely clear what errors a syllable segmentation strategy would predict. As described previously, the number of syllables in erroneously perceived words or phrases does not invariably correspond to their targets, nor would they be expected to in English.

The foregoing suggestion could be interpreted to predict that segments would not change their position within a syllable; that is, consonants in syllable onsets would never become associated with codas, and consonants in codas would never become onsets. Word boundary errors which involve

TABLE 6.10   Word Boundary and Unstressed Vowel Errors

setting up of time → studying of time

they had a ten-year party → a tenure party

Wouldn't she look good with a ring in her nose → oregano nose

I'll catch my breath here → catch my breakfast

the paramour → the power mower

kills germs where they grow → kills germs with egg roll

he got ten years in prison → tenure in prison

this nation → the station

TABLE 6.11   Word Boundary and Stress Errors

front vowels occur only in words → front vowels are Kyrolean words

I have to eat too → I have eighty-two

roll up the back window → patrol the back window

Geez, really? → Disraeli

Louisiana → New Zealand

no bullshit exams → noble shit exams

phonological restructuring provide relevant test materials. These errors did not provide much support for invariant segment positions in syllable structure. Some consonants assumed a syllable onset position when a following word lacked an onset:

> We could give them an ice bucket → a nice bucket
> this Acoustical Society → the Sacoustical Society.

Perhaps these examples would follow from the prediction, under the assumption that a consonant vowel (CV) syllable is more likely than a syllable beginning with a vowel. However, when words began with more than one consonant, the word boundary shift was as likely to complicate the syllable onset as to simplify it. The example

> I scream → ice cream

is just the reverse of

> I need a loose crew → loose screw.

And in the example

> good old zebra's law → zebra slaw

a word-final fricative is perceived as initial, creating a complex syllable onset, while in

> a bee flying backward → a beef lying backward

a fricative which was a member of a complex syllable onset was perceived as word final.

There were also a number of examples of reordering which altered the position of segments within syllables, though reordering of segments seldom crossed syllable or word boundaries. These are repeated from Chapter 4 in Table 6.12.

The slips are consistent with the suggestions of Cutler et al. (1989) that English listeners do not use syllables for primary segmentation.

6.7. INFERENCES ABOUT THE LEXICON

Because it is possible for listeners to report hearing nonwords, they must be able to develop a phonological representation of the phonetic stream which is casual speech. In all likelihood, the segmentation of the phonetic stream involves reference to stressed syllables and stressed syllables may also provide reliable information for initiating lexical access. Unstressed syllables and unstressed function words seem not to provide reliable information either for word boundaries or for syntactic function. The errors are consistent with the idea that affixes and contracted forms have some independence within the lexicon.

TABLE 6.12   Misorderings Crossing Syllable and Word Boundaries

---

Across a syllable boundary

Acton Road → Atkin Road

without your mother along → without your mother-in-law

frothing → throfing

Across a word boundary

found a copy → pound of coffee

spun toffee → fun stocking

I'm making boats → taking notes

she wants to be a teacher → she wants me to teach her

roll up the back window → patrol the back window

my three-ninety class → my three-D night class

CHAPTER 7

Syntax

[R]emarkably sparse stimulation can lead to rich perception . . .

—Noam Chomsky (1996)

Because many of the misperceptions were short and fragmentary portions of sentences, the sample does not provide a great deal of material for analysis of syntactic misperceptions. In addition, the longer a misperception is, the more likely is its report influenced by memory rather than reflecting only perceptual processes. Even with the limitations of a small database of uncertain reliability, some interesting observations can be made at the level of phrases if not often at the level of sentences.

7.1. GRAMMATICALITY

Some misperceptions appeared to be motivated by considerations of syntactic well-formedness. In these slips, function words were reported as needed for grammatical sentences; that is, they showed editing. Some examples follow:

In four to six months we'll get a house → four to six marks will get you a house
I was through on a bus → I was thrown off a bus
It'll be a confusing weekend → You're confusing weekends

I've never cooked anybody's goose → cooked anybody mouse
Is that home baked? → Is that hard to bake?
attacks in the ear → a tax on the ear.

The addition of *you* in the first example, the perception of *on* as *off* in the second example and of *in* as *on* in the sixth, the loss of the article in the third, and of the possessive marker in the fourth all appear to be required to make the resulting perception grammatical. Which proportion of the changes in grammatical structure are purely perceptual and which are influenced by memory and the attempt to report a misperception is impossible to say.

It is possible that the adjustments in the following had a similar source, an attempt to preserve grammatical structure:

> I'll catch my breath here → catch my breakfast
> kills germs where they grow → kills germs with egg roll
> those shoes → oh shoot
> Is he nasty? → Is he an ass?

Since the meaning of a proportion of the errors was strange or unlikely, it seems that grammatical structure has some perceptual reality even when the content of the whole communication has undergone improbable revision.

Although most of the time the syntactic structure of the misperception reported was well-formed, there were examples in which part of speech assignment lead to impossible or nearly impossible structures. The following are some of these examples:

> I'm staying near O'Hare → more O'Hare
> we offered six → we Alfred six
> I'm conking out → coffee out
> I know what happened to our ice, Andy → to high Sandy
> A friend of ours is having a lung removed → is having alumni move
> My handout isn't as good as I hoped it would be → I told it would be.
> I just got back from Denison → back from dentist
> I'll catch my breath here → my brushup
> Wouldn't she look good with a ring in her nose? → oregano nose

The examples vary in how likely they are to be judged ungrammatical. The ones with missing articles may simply reflect an inaccurate or incomplete report of the misperception. The most deviant example seems to be

> we offered six → we Alfred six,

in which a verb is replaced by a proper name without any adjustment of the remainder of the phrase.

A cautionary note is in order. Although we tend to think that the speech which listeners must process is composed primarily of grammatical sentences, we do not know to what extent this is true. Listeners certainly hear grammatical sentences as well as phrases, false starts, and ungrammatical utterances. Exactly what proportion of each of these listeners expect to hear and what proportion they will accept is not known. Listener expectations concerning the completeness and grammaticality of ordinary speech must interact with their reports of slips of the ear.

7.2. CONSTITUENT BOUNDARIES AND CONSTITUENT STRUCTURE

Any model of sentence understanding would require that a listener locate constituents in the stream of speech, that is, find constituent boundaries, and assign or develop a structure showing the relationships between constituents. Fodor and Bever (1965) have argued for the hypothesis that major sentence constituents are perceptual units, stating that "[t]he unit of speech perception corresponds to the constituent" (p. 415). A slightly different version of this idea is presented by Bever, Lackner, and Kirk (1969).

If major constituents are perceptual units, they should resist destruction. Consequently, we would not expect word boundary errors or errors in the order of segments to cross major constituent boundaries.

7.2.1. CONSTITUENT BOUNDARIES AND ORDER ERRORS

There are only four examples in which ordering errors were associated with constituent boundaries in some way:

> I have to eat too → I have eighty-two
> She wants to be a teacher → She wants me to teach her
> without your mother along → without your mother-in-law
> my three-ninety class → my three-D night class.

None of these provided a clear example of misordering across a major constituent boundary. The data, therefore, support the idea that syntactic constituents are perceptual units which resist decomposition.

The slips do not distinguish between two possible sources of perceptual unity of syntactic constituents. It is possible that unity is a result of syntactic structure. It is also possible that constituents are organized as intonational phrases and that phonological cues such as pauses, pitch contours, and preboundary lengthening are responsible for the coherence of syntactic constituents.

Although most slips seem to retain their overall phrasing and intonation patterns, there are a few exceptions:

> Mom, he did it → Mommy did it
> Sonic, the hedgehog → son of the hedgehog
> I know what happened to our ice, Andy → to high Sandy
> Geez, really? → Disraeli.

In each of these slips, a phonological phrase boundary is lost. Two of the lost boundaries involve a form of direct address: one is an exclamation, and one involves a proper name with a phrase used in apposition as an explanation or definition. Because the exceptions to the general pattern are somewhat marginal, it seems likely that intonation and phrasing provide a structure or scaffolding which guides listener perception of sentences.

7.2.2. CONSTITUENT BOUNDARIES AND WORD BOUNDARIES

Just as errors in the order of segments or syllables did not appear to occur across major constituent boundaries, so errors in word boundary assignment typically did not cross major constituent boundaries either. The examples in which word boundary errors crossed constituent boundaries were few and not entirely convincing. The following are examples which do not depend on radical phonetic restructuring:

> We're going to pour him into the car → purim into the car
> Mom, he did it → Mommy did it
> urination → you're a nation
> I scream → ice cream
> everything's about a quarter more → about a quart or more
> a bee flying backward → a beef lying backward

The number of examples such as this is small. The *I scream* → *ice cream* example may have been influenced by folklore through the children's rhyme "I scream, you scream, we all scream for ice cream." Only one example, the last, clearly involves a major constituent boundary. This misperception occurred in the context of a riddle:

> *Question:* What goes "zzub, zzub, zzub"?
> *Answer:* A bee flying backward.

Perhaps the listener was prepared to suspend normal expectations when faced with an odd question. On the other hand, there are examples of misperceptions which alter constituent structure radically but only in association with other errors. These are given in Table 7.1 (below, in Section 7.4).

7.2.3. REINTERPRETATION OF CONSTITUENTS

There were many examples of reinterpretations of constituents. The examples give an indication of the possibilities rather than an exhaustive list.

Major constituents such as noun phrase (NP) and verb phrase (VP) were misidentified, for example,

<u>NP becomes NPVP</u>

IREX → I was

structure, style and usage → instruct your style and usage

<u>NPVP becomes VP</u>

no she isn't → no shitting

<u>NP plus V becomes NP</u>

I'm going to try to get it towed → to get a toad

<u>NP becomes infinitive</u>

Mary, would you like some tea with this? → to eat with us.

Within major constituents, there were a great many errors which affected conjoined NP's. In these, the conjunction *and* was typically reinterpreted as an unstressed syllable of the first conjoint:

<u>NP and NP becomes NP</u>

Sara Garnes and Ilse → Sara Garnes Nielsen

cinema and photography → cinnamon photography

he works in an herb and spice shop → an urban spice shop

a purse and a billfold → a personal billfold

fruits and vegetables → prudent vegetables

The reverse error—introducing a conjunction so that a conjoint was created—was less frequent:

<u>NP becomes NP *and* NP</u>

Jefferson Starship → Jeffers and starship

He's an ENT → an E and T

Related to these were intermediate errors such as

he and Annie's father → he and his father.

Within verb phrases, similar structural changes appeared to be possible. Verbs with following object NPs were interpreted as simple verbs. Less commonly, simple verbs were partitioned into two constituents. Infinitive phrases were reinterpreted as other constituents:

V plus NP becomes V
just bisecting lines → just bicycling
You're not wearing one → not married
missed the news → must a snoozed

V becomes V plus NP
Ann was afraid to go → afraid to do it

Infinitives
with less than two weeks to go → less than two weeks ago
I have to eat too → I have eighty-two

Modifiers and prepositional phrases were reinterpreted as constituents of various types:

Prepositional phrases
the floor of the house → the Florida house
I don't intend to stay in the picture → to stain the picture
I have them do out-of-class writing → auto class writing

Modifier structure
she's ripe → she's raped
an errand to run near High Street → to run on New High Street
You've got all the books you need for the time being → for your typing
This friend of ours who visited → of ours is an idiot
I don't think of the bass as a solo instrument → as so low an instrument
kills germs where they grow → kills germs with egg roll
I tripped on a tent pole → tadpole

The limits on reinterpreting constituents are not at all clear. In particular, there was no one property or characteristic of the utterance which invariably survived, providing reliable syntactic information.

7.3. SUBCATEGORIZATION

Beginning with the work of Fodor, Garrett, and Bever (1968), a great deal of the literature dealing with parsing sentences has been devoted to the subcategorization of verbs (Gorrell, 1991). That is, whether a verb may be followed by an NP direct object (*John bought a book*), two NPs (*Mary sent John a book*), or a sentence complement (*John believed that Mary loved him*) or does not allow any complements (*John slept*) is a property of the verb itself. Listeners presumably use complement frames associated with verbs to guide their expectations and their subsequent analyses of the syntactic structure of sentences.

This hypothesis would predict that errors in the perception of a verb which changed the verb's subcategorization frame would lead to further errors in the syntactic analysis of the verb's complements. More generally, errors in a major syntactic category which imposes particular structural requirements should cascade into following material.

There are a few slips which seem to show cascading requirements:

Auxilliaries

missed the news → must a snoozed
It'll be a confusing weekend → You're confusing weekends

Verb complements

Ann was afraid to go → afraid to do it
teach someone to act → Do you know a rat?
I'm going to go back to bed until the news → I'm going to go back to bed and crush the noodles

These examples involve considerable restructuring of phonological material. They are consistent with the hypothesis that an error in assigning a syntactic category to one word affects following words.

The first two examples above show the effects of misperceived auxilliary verbs. In the first, the article *the* was perceived as an auxilliary *have,* which requires a verb form to follow it. The verb *snoozed* was reported, as required. The second example is similar in that the modal auxilliary *will* was perceived as a form of *be* and the following material was interpreted as the appropriate VP.

In the next three examples above, an intransitive verb was perceived as a transitive verb and the required direct object was reported. An intransitive *go* was perceived as a transitive *do,* and the required direct object *it* was supplied. The erroneously perceived verb *know* requires a direct object, and the remaining phonological material was reinterpreted as the required direct object NP, *a rat.* The last example involves more radical phonological restructuring, but it also seems to involve an intransitive verb analyzed as a transitive with phonological material reinterpreted as the required direct object, *the noodles.* In the misperception

John's nose is on crooked → John knows his own cooking,

a noun *nose* was interpreted as a verb and the following material was reinterpreted as an appropriate complement. The error is also consistent with experimental results which show that listeners are sensitive to all phonologically appropriate lexical candidates, regardless of part-of-speech requirements (Tanenhaus, Leiman, & Seidenberg, 1979).

Although there are only a few such examples, the appealing idea that the syntactic requirements established by one word guide the analysis of following words is consistent with the slips data.

7.4. RADICAL RESTRUCTURING

Finally, there were a number errors that are best simply listed. All these errors involve quite radical changes of the phonology, syntax, and semantics of an utterance. In particular, the semantic interpretation is often inappropriate or silly. However, the overall rhythmic pattern of the target and the misperception is maintained. These slips are given in Table 7.1.

Related to radical restructuring is one example of a cross-linguistic misperception. The listener was a native speaker of Latvian and a proficient speaker of English. She was making a telephone call to a university department in order to make contact with a visitor from Latvia. The speaker answered the phone, giving *ceramics,* the name of the department in the Fine-Arts Building. The listener heard *saimnieks,* Latvian for "farmer." The misperception has a phonological resemblance to the surname of the visitor, Podnieks, which was probably uppermost in the listener's mind. It also crosses language boundaries. There are no other examples of errors of this type in the data set.

7.5. GENERAL PROPERTIES OF THE PERCEPTION OF SYNTAX

If we examine the set of slips providing information about the perception of syntactic structure, we can draw several conclusions.

First, there is a tendency to report—and perhaps to perceive—grammatical rather than deviant phrases and sentences. Ungrammatical phrases and sentences are possible, though rare.

Second, although parts of constituents can be reinterpreted in misperception, there is a strong tendency for major constituent boundaries to be maintained, that is, for major constituents to act as perceptual units. This unity is based on phonological and syntactic properties, though because almost all slips

TABLE 7.1   Weird and Wonderful Slips of the Ear

Do you want a grape? → a drink

Making Polish pisanki → Polish prosody

a red jacket → a red cap

theraputic hibachi → computer hibachi

they were going to Akron → to Africa

What's happening? → What's that mean?

a ride with Dr. von Gierke → in a brown derby

with drugs → at stud

Parcheesi set → Parmesan cheese

Friar Tuck pizza → Kentucky Fried pizza

typewriter → card table

After the rubber boat had been wrecked in the squall → After the rubber boot had been erected in the squirrel

You could light a small house with him → reminds you of Householder

living with a coach → women who coach

College Outline Grammar of French → how to jabber in French

I read three articles and that's about it → I read three articles on phonetics

Are you going to have a baby? → Are you going out with David?

energy from the sun → hemorrhaging from the side

I didn't think he would let us use his car → I didn't think he'd last through the day

fixing sausage → fish sticks

discussions before tomorrow → discussions of Borg-Warner

Sorry, kid, but you're not mine → It's your kid, not mine

Oh, The Great Escape → Oh, Fred Astaire

How've you been? → Got a minute?

I wasn't getting anywhere with all those vowel adjustments → with all those bottles of aspirin

I seem to be thirsty → I sing through my green Thursday

I have a headache → I haven't had any

prove some statement of Scriptures → prove some structural descriptions

I'm going to go back to bed until the news → I'm going to go back to bed and crush the noodles

They took footprints when you're born → They took footprints in the dorm

pecan log → common law

I'm gonna try and get home before it rains → I'm gonna try to get hold of Fort Wayne

What else? → mayonnaise

bear country → Erica

That's the mother in me → that's the multirunway

(Continues)

126

TABLE 7.1 *(Continued)*

Did you check off roast duck? → something was froze stuck

a linguini is a noodle → a lean Wheatie is a noodle

never enough → mother him up

the guy was there with the Indian cigarettes → the guy ordered VD and cigarettes

teach someone to act → Do you know a rat?

what the difference in the Bedouin case is → in the better one is

Orange Julius → on through no and yes

Art Garfunkel → our current fumble

John's nose is on crooked → John knows his own cooking

and your next appearance will be at Santa Laura College → as a saddle or a carriage

You sure like your booze → You don't like your boots

the Clemency Information Center → the Columbus Information Center

What's happening? → seven

I'm gonna go home and work on my income tax → mop and wax

It's happy Hudy time → It's *Howdy Doody* time

clash of the titans → or else they're fighting

farmer financier → thin man here

Old Navy store → oak baby store

maintain phonological phrasing to some degree, it seems that phrasing provides the overall scaffolding which listeners employ in perception.

Third, the syntactic requirements of one lexical item seem to guide the syntactic analysis of following lexical items and even lead to perceived words which are necessary to fill a syntactic subcategorization frame.

Finally, the semantic content of slips seems to be unconstrained. As has often been observed, grammar allows us to say and understand the unexpected.

CHAPTER **8**

Summary and Conclusions

[S]peech perception depends on perceptual analysis and cognitive structure alike.
—Robert E. Remez et al. (1994)

8.1. PERCEPTUALLY SALIENT PROPERTIES

The corpus of errors is large enough to allow generalizations about what is and what is not likely to be lost or changed when a slip of the ear occurs. The most straightforward interpretation of the data is that properties which are seldom misperceived are perceptually salient, providing reliable or useful information to listeners. Properties which are repeatedly lost or altered are less salient and less useful. Listeners are likely to fill in these properties from knowledge about the language, the speaker, and the conversation.

Most perceptual errors were complicated rather than simple, affecting more than one aspect of utterances. Individual segments differed in saliency, so that some segment types and positions were more likely than others to be misperceived.

8.1.1. The Phonetic Structure of Adult Slips

There were few vowel errors. Front vowels were more likely to be misperceived than back vowels, and the typical misperception affected vowel height. There were few errors in the perception of stress patterns.

Consonant additions and substitutions typically occurred in initial or final position rather than medially. This distribution characterized both simple and complex misperceptions. The most favored environment for consonant loss was final position, particularly a final consonant cluster. The perception of spurious consonants, consonant additions, was less common than perceptual loss of consonants.

It should be noted that the tendency for errors to occur word-initially and -finally may be as much a result of the types of words found in the corpus as of a perceptual tendency. A majority of the words which served as perceptual targets were one-syllable words which allow only initial or final consonants but not medial consonants to serve as targets.

In substitutions, obstruents served as targets more often than did resonants. In general, obstruents were perceived as obstruents and resonants as resonants, suggesting that fundamental manner categories are resistant to confusion. This finding is compatible with the suggestion of Dalby, Laver, and Hiller (1986) that phonemes form midclass categories confusable within but not across categories. There did not appear to be any pronounced preferences for place of articulation errors, either as targets or as substitutions.

Typically, syllables were perceptually added or lost in final position. The affected syllables were almost always unstressed. Added or lost words were function words, unstressed in sentence context. Errors in word boundary placement—loss, addition, or shift—also typically involved unstressed function words. The affected function words were usually part of a phonological phrase with neighboring content words.

Misordering of portions of utterances was most likely to take place within syllables. Misorderings did not respect the organization of syllables into onsets and rimes, as slips of the tongue tend to do.

8.1.2. The Phonetic Structure of Child Slips

The sort of errors observed for children suggest that their speech perception processes are very similar to adult processes. Children made few vowel errors. Front vowels were the most likely targets, and the error involved vowel height. There was a tendency for front–back errors to affect lax vowels. Children showed the same error types for consonants as adults did, that is, additions, loss, and substitutions. There were relatively few additions but many substitutions. The substitutions were typically obstruents for obstruents and resonants for resonants, just as in the adult data. Consonants were most likely to be lost in final position.

Syllable loss was much more common than syllable addition. The missing syllables were unstressed, often in final position. A number of these syllables were composed of liquids, which can sometimes be syllabic and sometimes not, depending on the utterance.

Children appeared to operate with less knowledge of their language than did adults, as indicated by a higher proportion of perceived nonwords and fewer misperceptions based on regular phonological reductions.

8.2. PHONOLOGY

Linguists have traditionally been concerned with the relationship between the phonetic details of an utterance and its phonological representation. Many linguists argue that phonological representations should mirror the feelings of native speakers for their language. Sapir (1921, p. 56) contrasts the phonetic and the phonological facts:

> In watching my Nootka interpreter write his language, I often had the curious feeling that he was transcribing an ideal flow of phonetic elements which he heard, inadequately from a purely objective standpoint, as the intention of the actual rumble of speech.

The discrepancy between phonetic facts and phonological reality which Sapir characterized in this famous passage has received comment from linguists working in different traditions from quite different points of view. In describing English stress, Lehiste (1970, p. 150) accepts the idea that "a person who knows the language 'hears' the predicted phonetic shapes" whether or not they are physically present in any detail.

Hockett (1987, p. 49) echoes Sapir:

> A linguistically accurate record . . . would have shown . . . WHAT THE INFOR-MANT THOUGHT SHE SAID—which is to say, what she heard herself say when saying the words with clarity-norm enunciation, not the actual sound but that sound INTERPRETED in terms of the articulatory-acoustic targets at which she was aiming.

Donegan and Stampe (1979) put the idea most succinctly: "The discrepancy between the sound perceived and intended, and the sound pronounced, is simply phonology" (p. 130).

A similar conclusion is found in the psycholinguistic literature (Remez, Rubin, Berns, Pardo, & Lang, 1994, p. 152):

> [N]o acoustic element plays an essential role in perception, and the acoustic grit of speech must merely provide the opportunity for a listener to detect perceptually crucial properties of spectro-temporal variation.

These impressions correspond to the impressions created by the misperception data. Listeners' perceptions appeared to be guided by their expectations about the phonology of English.

First, the inventory of reported segments was (with one exception) the English inventory. Some of the speakers spoke with foreign accents, yet though the accents may have led to perceptual errors, they did not lead to perceived non-English segments. In casual speech, segments occur with are not part of the English phonological inventory. For example, voiceless laterals and rhotics occur when /l/ and /r/ follow aspirated voiceless stops; nasalized vowels commonly precede nasal consonants. Although some of the listeners were bilingual and almost all were familiar with other languages, none of them reported non-English phonological segments.

Second, the adult misperceptions were invariably phonologically well-formed according to English phonotactics or morpheme structure rules. In casual speech, not only do segments occur which are not part of the English inventory, but also sequences occur which violate phonotactic constrains. For example, reduced vowels may be deleted in the first syllable of both words such as *Celeste* (former governor of Ohio) producing /slɛst/ and in words such as *serene* producing /srin/, the latter not being a possible morpheme. Yet adult listeners did not report any non-English sequences (see Fokes & Bond, 1993).

Third, listeners compensated for low-level phonological rules, such as flapping and cluster simplification, when compensation was not necessary. That is, listeners operated as if phonology guided their analysis of reduced, or supposedly reduced, utterances.

8.3. LEXICAL AND SYNTACTIC KNOWLEDGE

Slips of the ear provide information about the ways lexical knowledge and the acoustic signal interact from two points of view: errors suggest the strategies which listeners use to segment continuous speech into words and phrasal units, and errors provide information about lexical access and organization.

Stressed syllables are strongly implicated in adult segmentation strategies. Listeners tend to assume that stressed syllables begin content words, and they tend to treat unstressed syllables as continuations of content words or as function words. Children may be less proficient in using this segmentation strategy than adults.

Syntactic phrases are treated as perceptual units. Perceptual unity is supported by prosodic organization. Even slips which involve radical restructuring of an utterance maintain a global rhythmic similarity of the targets with their misperceptions.

Content words are accessed from the reliable information provided by stressed syllables. Words are not accessed syllable by syllable or segment by segment. Rather, strong and weak syllables have quite different perceptual saliency. Words may be accessed on the bases of global similarities in acoustic properties distributed over a stretch of speech. Function words undergo frequent restructuring or editing, as grammatical context demands. Content words are adjusted less readily. Some morphologically complex words are probably represented as separate morphemes in the lexicon.

Finally, listeners report the perception of nonexisting words, suggesting that phonological representation can on occasion be independent of lexical knowledge.

8.4. IMPLICATIONS FOR LINGUISTIC THEORY

Zwicky (1982) examined the connection between performance data—in his example, his collection of "classical malapropisms"—and linguistic theory. Zwicky concluded that the "data bear only at great remove and in a limited way on issues of linguistic theory" (p. 131).

The same has to be said for slips of the ear. Misperceptions are errors which take place during language use; that is, they are performance errors. Linguistic theory attempts to describe the knowledge underlying language use—linguistic competence. Until theories of competence incorporate principles which translate competence into performance, or vice versa, until performance models include linguistic competence, it is nearly impossible to use data obtained in one domain to evaluate claims made in the other.

The most that can be done is to provide examples of errors which are consistent with the idea that listeners act as if they had access to particular kinds of linguistic knowledge.

8.5. IMPLICATIONS FOR MODELS OF LANGUAGE USE

Slips of the ear undoubtedly occur under conditions of multiple causation. For some, phonetic and/or phonological explanations seem plausible. Other errors with no obvious phonetic cause may have multiple explanations in the external and internal environment of the listeners, their mental state, interests, abilities, and many other factors difficult to either specify or assess. In addition, listeners' attention may be engaged in different ways while they are listening to speech. In many conversational situations, listeners are also performing other activities, so perceptual errors may also reflect allocation of attention. Sometimes listeners seem to be sensitive to the details of speech. At other times, listeners are content to rely on the most salient and accessible properties of the acoustic signal.

Nevertheless, it is possible to use the slips data to offer some suggestions about characteristics of the speech perception process.

Are there units in speech perception? The literature proposing and debating units is considerable and ultimately inconclusive. On the one hand, what listeners attend to in speech is a function of their task. In a phonetics class, listeners may be required to attend to every last fragment of phonetic information. In listening to the speech of young children, listeners attempt to recover words even when produced with considerable distortion. *Dwama, how dwos* can be reconstructed to mean "Grandma, how gross" and *top, top* can mean "Stop, stop." In the first case, listeners are focusing on phonetic detail; in the second, they are bypassing phonological information, using it as a bridge to meaning.

Experiments dealing with cues employed in speech perception are probably closer to the phonetics class extreme in listening; because of the variability of available information, ordinary conversation is closer to the other extreme. The slips data suggest that listeners are opportunistic, using any phonetic information that will lead them to recover or grasp the meaning intended by speakers. Listeners appear to rely on clearly articulated stressed vowels and segment classes. The information is not strictly sequential but rather distributed in time over a domain of at least a syllable, at most an intonational phrase. The slips data are consistent with the conclusions of Wright, Frisch, and Pisoni (1996/97), who argue that "there is no evidence for the primacy of any particular unit in perception. In fact, the perceptual task itself may determine the units that hearers use to analyze the speech signal" (p. 5).

Listeners must be able to connect phonological information with words in the mental lexicon. The question of units in perception therefore leads directly to the question of lexical representation. Because listeners sometimes report the perception of nonexistent words having a phonological form related to the phonetic information which they have heard, listeners must be able to construct phonological representations from phonetic input. We might argue, on the basis of simplicity, that if listeners are able to construct phonological representations on occasion, they do so routinely. In other words, the slips data support a representation of lexical items based on linguistic (symbolic) units rather than a representation based on prototypes built from episodic encounters with words (see Wright et al., 1996/97).

Assuming that lexical items have a phonological representation which listeners employ, the slips data and other data based on perceptual tasks (see Neel, Bradlow, & Pisoni, 1996/97) indicate that listeners treat stressed vowels as reliable information. However, it may be that information which is useful for access is different from information used in lexical representations. Van Ooijen

(1996), employing a postperceptual task, has found that listeners are more likely to change vowels than consonants in converting a nonword into a word: on the one hand, vowels are more intelligible than consonants; on the other, vowels are more readily disregarded than consonants when the listener is finding a lexical item from partially incorrect information. Clearly, different tasks are accessing different aspects of lexical representation. Properties of words used in access are not necessarily the same as properties which efficiently partition the lexical search space.

As Cutler and colleagues have demonstrated, segmentation—finding words in the stream of speech—is related to the structure of a language. The English slips data are consistent with Cutler and Norris's (1988) suggestion that listeners use strong or stressed syllables to initiate lexical search.

What might be the organization of the search space in the mental lexicon? How is phonological information mapped in the lexical search space? There are numerous and much debated models of lexical access and word recognition: some have been modeled computationally; others are based on psychological considerations (for reviews, see Lively, Pisoni, & Goldinger, 1994; Wright et al., 1996/97). Although the slips data can not definitively exclude any of the models, they suggest that listeners entertain multiple lexical candidates including, as suggested by Shillcock (1990), matches to portions of words. The cohort of candidates is not limited by part-of-speech restrictions or semantic appropriateness. Rather, the criterion for entertaining lexical candidates appears to be phonological similarity.

In modeling listener interpretation of syntactic structure, "it has not yet proved feasible to tap into the basic structure-building procedures which presumably underlie the entire process" (Mitchell, 1994, p. 376). Much of the experimental work deals with the effects of and the resolution of ambiguous structures. There are no examples in the slips data of the effects of syntactic ambiguity. Rather, the contribution of the data set is to point to the effect of intonational phrasing. The data suggest that the analysis of sentence structure is linked to prosody, to the intonational organization of phrases and sentences. [See Morgan and Demuth (1996) for extensive discussion of prosody in language acquisition.]

Finally, the slips data show that contextual predictability is not a strong constraint in language understanding. Rather, listeners are willing to entertain semantically wildly implausible utterances.

8.6. FUTURE RESEARCH

An issue which has recently emerged in psycholinguistics concerns the effect of specific linguistic structures in speech perception and language understanding.

Do listeners use different strategies in speaking and listening in different languages? This data set deals purely with the perception and understanding of English. Most other studies of slips of the ear have also described English errors. Slips of the ear are also available in German, a language which is typologically quite similar to English.

It would be extremely valuable to develop data sets of perceptual errors from other languages. Such cross-linguistic comparisons would enable us to understand the universal vs. the language specific in speech perception and language-understanding strategies. Psycholinguistics is comparatively healthy.

Experimental Errors

Are perceptual errors reported in conversation odd or unique? Or are these errors characteristic of speech processing? Can the observational data be validated to some degree by experimental data obtained under controlled circumstances? This question is easy to ask and has been repeatedly raised concerning the database used in this report. This appendix will describe a set of perceptual errors obtained under experimental control.

The data were obtained in connection with an experiment designed to compare the speech understanding abilities of native and nonnative listeners. Part of the experiment asked listeners to respond to standard sentences (Harvard sentences: see Egan, 1944) developed for intelligibility testing.

The sentences were recorded by five young males, native speakers of Midwestern American English. The sentences were presented to listeners in a clear condition as well as under various conditions of signal distortion, that is, filtering to match the bandwidth of telephone transmission and adding pink noise.

The listeners were young college students, native speakers of American English enrolled in a Midwestern university. Listeners heard the sentences over earphones in a quiet listening laboratory. They responded by either writing the sentences or by repeating them. The details of the experiment are reported in Bond, Moore, and Gable (1996).

The primary advantage of experimental conditions for eliciting perceptual errors is control of what the listeners hear. In naturalistic circumstances, both the perception and the target utterance are reported from memory. Potentially memory of one or the other or both is deficient. This problem does not arise when listeners are asked to respond to recorded speech. The listener responses were sometimes erroneous, and furthermore the response errors resembled errors observed in the perception of casual conversational speech. This finding is quite reassuring.

Yet there are problems with experimental data. First, the listeners were asked to respond by either writing or saying what they heard. Writing as a response mode is more dependent on memory than is speaking and introduces other sources of error. For example, written responses show spelling errors. Spelling errors are given in Table A.1. A portion of these are probably of no further interest except that they indicate that not all college students know the conventional orthography of English, a finding not particularly surprising. Another portion, however, suggests that listeners found a homonym or a near-homonym of the word they heard in the mental lexicon. There are also instances which are not clearly the one or the other.

A second problem concerns listening conditions. As one would expect, the more disruptive the listening conditions are, the more listener errors occur and the more destructive the errors are, in comparison with the target utterances. On the one hand, knowing the listening condition is important. On the other, such knowledge makes comparison with naturally occurring perceptual errors difficult because for these the listening conditions are not known, though they would tend to be more benign than some laboratory listening conditions.

A third problem, in fact the major problem, might be called listener compliance. The listeners found themselves in a situation in which they had to produce a response; they had to say something or write something down. They may have responded with guesses which reflect not perception but a response strategy. Naturally occurring slips are real in that listeners are not obliged to respond. When listeners report a slip of the ear, we can be sure that an error did occur since listeners do not have to volunteer anything at all.

TABLE A.1　Errors in Orthography

Orthographic errors
birch → The BURCH canoe
dope → John is just a DOP
breach → Soldiers poured through the wide BREECH in the wall (2×)
gnashed → The ape grinned and KNASHED his yellow teeth
reared → The colt RIRED and threw the sick rider

Selection of homonyms in the lexicon
Two → TO blue herring
the i → Put a dot on the EYE (2×)
bees → The ____ of B
tea → The planet TEE helps to test the evening

Note. The word which the listeners heard is given as the target. Multiple errors of the same type are identified (e.g., 2× indicates that the error occurred twice).

The experimental errors were classified as based either primarily on phonology or primarily on syntax and the lexicon. There were clear cases at either extreme, but there was also a middle ground in which errors appeared to be based primarily on one property but appeared to show traces of the other. In classifying errors, omissions were ignored as were fragmentary responses which could not be matched to parts of the target sentences.

Vowel Errors

Experimental errors which involved misreporting vowels with most of the target word reported correctly are given in Table A.2. There were few examples of pure vowel errors. A high proportion of the errors occurred in words with a syllable-final /r/, /l/ or nasals, a pattern similar to that found in natural slips. One error affected an unstressed syllable. The report of *drink* for *drank* was probably influenced by the listener's interpretation of the target sentence rather than being purely perceptual.

Consonant Errors

The same general error types occurred experimentally as in naturally occurring slips, namely, consonant addition, loss, and substitution. Simple substitutions were far more common than loss. There were few additions. In initial position, most errors affected obstruents and there was a tendency for obstruents to be replaced by obstruents. Manner, place, and voicing substitutions all occurred, though most commonly the error consonant differed from the target consonant on more than one dimension.

The substitution of *boy* for *coy* seems unlikely to be perceptual. *Coy* is a relatively unusual word and the context of the target sentence included *girl*, thus suggesting *boy* by association. The resonant errors, though listed here as a substitution, may also reflect listeners' tendencies to report a relatively common word *mashed* for the rarer word *gnashed*. Errors for consonants in initial position are given in Table A.3.

Since the experimental sentences tended to use monosyllabic words as targets, there were few opportunities for medial consonant errors. There was one possible simple error in the spoken response mode, a substitution for a medial consonant:

   useless → The first was full of YOUTH-ful trash.

If the /s/ in *use* was indeed misperceived, then the report of *ful* for *less* suggests that the listener selected a possible word from the lexicon on the basis of the first syllable.

TABLE A.2   Vowel Errors

Spoken response mode

dope → John is just the DUPE of long standing

our → Dig   marks the WAR efforts

          This   the end   AIR efforts

          the MORE effort

hum → The HEM of bees made Jim sleepy

wrist → The ROAST was badly strained and hung loon

          The ROOST was badly strained and hung limp

          The ROAST was badly strained and unlit

poured → Soldiers TORE through the white reef to the wall

groaned → The age GRANED and gnashed his yellow teeth

drank → DRINK a coke with rum therein

fail → He was bribed to cause the new motor to FEEL

Unstressed syllable

herring → Two blue HERONS swam

Written response mode

well → It's easy to tell the depth of a WHALE

hum → The HYMN of bees made Jim sleepy

colt → The CULT retired and threw the sick rider

coat → Mend the CUT before you go out

wrist → The ROAST was badly strained

          The ROAST was badly strained and hung limp

coy → The KOW girl gave no green response

          The QUAY girl gave no clear response

poured → Soldiers PORED through the wide   in the wall

coat → The frosty air passed through the KITE (2×)

drank → DRINK a coke with rum therein

air → The CUR passed through the coat

woman → Help the WOMEN get back to her feet

Unstressed syllable

herring → Two blue HERON swam in the sink

TABLE A.3   Errors for Consonants in Initial Position

Written response mode

Substitutions for obstruents

planks → The birch canoe slid on the bare BANKS

birch → PERCH through the

bowls → round MOLE

bore → The stray cat WORE green boots

tea → The planet V helps the pair beneath me

The planet Z helps beneath me

The pun in P helps to pass the evening

A pint of PEA helps to pass the ET

The planet P helps to pass the E thing

The planet P helped

coy → The BOY and girl gave no response

The BOY   gave no clear response

The BOY and girl gave no

What TOY did

verse → Please FIRST out loud for pleasure

Read FIRST out loud for pleasure

sue → TO the bank under a false name

thrown → Check the PHONE by the parked truck

chills → A cry in the night KILLS

Substitutions for resonants

gnashed → The ape grinned and MASHED his yellow teeth (5×)

The ape screamed and MASHED his yellow teeth

The ape ran and MASHED the yellow key

reared → The cold VERED through the sick rider

read → WE verse out loud for pleasure

Consonant added

eel → The VEAL tastes sweet but looks awful

air → The frosty HAIR passed through the coat

The CUR passed through the coat

lack → The smoky fires BLACK flame and heat

A smoky fire's BLACK flame and heat

Smoky fires and BLACK heat

our → the MORE effort

gnashed → The ape grinned and FLASHED his yellow teeth

(Continues)

TABLE A.3 *(Continued)*

Ordering

tastes → An eel STATES sweet but looks awful

Spoken response mode

Obstruents

planks → The birch canoe slid on the smooth BANKS

purse → The FIRST was full of youthful trash

The FIRST was full of useful trash

pest → TESTS may be a man or a disease

TEST may be a man or a disease

A TEST may be a man or entity

buy → For quick cleaning FIVE

coy → The boy gave no clear response

sue → DO the bank under expulsination

Resonants

gnashed → The ape screamed   MASHED

wide → Soldiers poured   RIDE break

Consonant added

our → Dig   marks the WAR efforts

Consonant lost

juice → USE of lemons makes fine punch

Errors affecting consonants in final position are given in Table A.4. Substitutions involved place, manner, and voicing, and they affected obstruents exclusively. A very high proportion of substitutions in final position as well as additions and deletions involved morphological readjustments, typically noun plurals or the past tense of verbs. These are probably best considered "editing" errors rather than perceptual errors. Their properties are quite similar to natural morphological slips in that inflectional suffixes were adjusted without affecting stems.

Consonant errors affecting clusters are given in Table A.5. Most commonly, consonant clusters were simplified, sometimes with accompanying substitution for one of the members. Less commonly, members of consonant clusters were reported as substitutions. Adding consonants to clusters was rare. As in errors

TABLE A.4   Errors for Consonants in Final Position

<u>Written response mode</u>

Substitutions for obstruents

colt → The COLD through the sick rider

The COLD reared and threw the sick rider

The COLD reared and BLEW the sick rider

sheet → Glue the SHEEP to the dark blue background

Lure the SHEEP to the dark blue background

Move the SHEEP with the dreadful background

Though the SHEEP to the dark

slid → The burch canoe SLIP on the smooth planks

wide → Soldiers tore through the WHITE reef to the wall

Soldiers forged through the WHITE   on the wall

birch → The BIRD   up the tree top

reef → The ship was torn apart on the sharp WREATH

maze → The crooked MAID failed to pull it off

The crooked MAID failed to fold the map

The crooked MAID failed to fool the

Consonant is added

glue → MOVE the sheet to the drawer in the back

MOVE the sheet to the dark blue background

MOVE the sheep to the   background

verse → Please FIRST out loud for pleasure

Read FIRST out loud for pleasure

Consonant is lost

stunned → The beauty of the view STUNG the young boy

bribed → His BRIDE caused the new motor to fail

chest → CHECK the phone by the parked truck

CHECK the girl beside the parked car

CHECK the road beside you park the truck

CHECK with

bowls → Write cross the word around the BONE

Reordering

pest → PETS may be a man or deed

(*Continues*)

TABLE A.4   (*Continued*)

Inflectional affixes affected

helps → The pint of tea HELPED pass the evening (4×)

             The planet HELPED to pass the evening

             The planet P HELPED

chills → A cry in the night CHILLED my marrow (4×)

fail → He was bribed because the new motor had FAILED

             He was fired because the new motor had FAILED

             because the new motor had FAILED

             He was bribed the cause the new motor that FAILED

smooth → SMOOTHED up planks

pest → PESTS may be a man or a disease (5×)

reef → The ship was torn apart on the sharp REEFS

wall → Soldiers poured through the wide breach in the WALLS (2×)

buzzard → This soup tastes like stewed BUZZARDS

fires → Smoky FIRE meant flame and heat

Spoken response mode

Substitutions

sheet → Two SHEEP were dark in the background

          Throw the SHEEP to the dark blue background

coat → The frosty air passed through the COACH (2×)

wide → Soldiers poured through the WHITE breach in the wall

          Soldiers poured WHITE break

          Soldiers poured   WHITE in the wall

          Soldiers poured   WHITE breeze in the wall

maze → The crooked MAID failed to fool the man (2×)

          The crooked MAID failed to fool the nun

false → Sue the bank under a FAULT

breach → Soldiers poured   white BREEZE in the wall

Consonant is lost

chest → CHECK

          CHECK was thrown by the parked truck

Consonant is added

glue → MOVE the sheet to the dark blue background (2×)

          MOVE the sheet in the dark blue background

days → Deep-BASED chicken LEGS are a rare dish

(*Continues*)

TABLE A.4   *(Continued)*

---

purse → The FIRST was full of youthful trash
                   The FIRST was full of useful trash

buy → For quick cleaning FIVE

Ordering

pest → Pets may be a man or a disease

Affixes affected

chills → The cry in the night CHILLED by marrow

helps → A pint of tea HELPED to pass the evening (3×)
                   of tea HELPED pass the evening

leg → These days chicken LEGS are a rare dish
                   Deep-based chicken LEGS are a rare dish

flame → Smoky fires lack FLAMES and heat

herring → Two blue HERRINGS swam in the sink

it → IT'S snowed, rained, and hailed the same morning

buzzard → This soup tastes like stewed BUZZARDS

efforts → This marks the end of our EFFORT

hands → Never kill a snake with your bare HAND

chickens → Mesh wire keeps CHICKEN inside

looks → An eel tastes sweet but LOOKED awful

---

affecting singleton consonants, affixes were common targets for errors. It is possible that the error

glue → BLUE the sheet to the dark blue background

resulted from confusion in reporting the sentence, giving the word *blue* both where appropriate and as a substitute for the target *glue*. In the error

strained → The wrist was badly SPRAINED and,

the substituted word is semantically appropriate and probably more likely from context.

Syllables

Errors involving changes in the number of syllables were rare without considerable restructuring, that is, substituting or adding lexical items. In the

TABLE A.5   Consonant Errors in Clusters

<u>Written response mode</u>

Substitution for one member

glue → BLUE the sheet to the dark blue background

                BLUE sheet with a dart blue background

purse → Her PULSE was full of useless trash

strained → The wrist was badly SPRAINED and (2×)

Simplification

roast → The ROAD was badly frayed and unopen

bribed → He was FIRED because the new motor had to fail

                  He was FIRED because the new motor had failed

glue → LURE the sheep to the dark blue background

wrist → The RIP was badly straight and hung low

chest → CHECK with

Affixes

bowls → Right or wrong it is not served in a brown BOWL

                Craig did not deserve a ROUND BOWL

marks → This MARKED the end of our efforts

stunned → The beauty of the view STUNG the young boy

<u>Spoken response mode</u>

Substitution for one member

strained → The wrist was badly SPRAINED

Simplification

glue → DO the sheet with the dark blue background

         TWO sheep were dark in the background

         LOOSE the sheet to the dark blue background

chest → The CHECK was thrown beside the parked truck

         CHECK

         CHECK was thrown by the parked truck

plunge → Hop over   PUNGE

stewed → This   like DEWED

planks → The birch canoe slid on the smooth BANKS

grinned → The ape REAMED and gnashed his yellow teeth

limp → The wrist was badly strained and hung LAP

Consonant added

thrown → The chest was STREWEN beside the parked truck

written response mode, there were only two examples of a word being reported with an extra syllable:

> **reared** → The cult RETIRED and threw the sick rider
> **stunned** → The beauty of the view STARTLED the young boy.

Syllable loss was more common. In the written response mode, there were several examples:

> **buzzard** → This soup tastes like stewed BUGS (2×)
>   This soup tastes like stewed BUZZED
> **frosty air** → The CUR passed through the coat
> **marrow** → A cry in the night chills my HAIR.

In the spoken response mode, one of the two examples of syllable loss was the same as in the written response mode:

> **buzzard** → This tastes like stewed BUGS
>   tastes like stewed BUGS
> **disease** → A pest may be a man or THIEF (2×)

All the errors in syllable number also have some semantic basis. Though syllable number was certainly not invariant, as indicated by more extreme restructuring of the target sentence, errors affecting primarily syllables within lexical items were rare.

Substitutions for Content Words

Content word substitutions were in part based on phonological information but also were influenced by semantics. The listeners knew they needed a word in a particular part of an utterance and simply reported a word that occurred to them. These examples, above all, demonstrate listener compliance. Because there was often some phonological similarity between the target and the substitute, it is difficult to say which examples are products of pure guesswork and which make the best use of limited phonological information. At least some of these may equally well have been classified as involving consonant and vowel substitutions.

Examples which suggest pure guesswork are the following:

> **rug** → For quick cleaning, buy a BRUSH
>   For quick cleaning, buy a BROOM
> **birch** → The BIRD up the tree top.

In the second example, the word *birch* is reported as *bird*, then a phrase associated with birds is reported without any phonological support in the target sentence.

Some responses seem to show contamination from other words in target sentences. In the error

view → The beauty of the ʀᴜɢ stunned the young boy,

the word *rug* is probably reported because it occurred in the sentence preceding the target, a more extreme example of the repetition of the word *blue* twice within one sentence. The substitution of *limb* in

wrist → The ʟɪᴍʙ was badly strained and hung limp

may also show contamination from *limp*.

There are a number of examples of substitutions of related words or near-synonyms. Apparently, listeners accessed the mental lexicon to the point of understanding the message but failed to remember the target word. They found a convenient synonym which expresses a similar idea. This type of error is also reported by Voss (1984). Some examples which illustrate this response type are the following:

stunned → The beauty of the view sᴛᴀʀᴛʟᴇᴅ the young boy
fool → The crooked maze failed to ᴄᴏɴғᴜsᴇ the mouse
crooked → The ᴘᴇʀғᴇᴄᴛ maze failed to fool the mouse.

Probably related to this phenomenon is a tendency for substituted lexical items to maintain their syntactic role. It is possible to match almost all the substitutes to subjects, verbs, or objects in the target sentences. Listeners seem to know where a lexical item is required in their response and fill in the blank as best they can.

Errors in the spoken response mode seem to be less affected by pure guesswork or contamination, suggesting that errors reported in writing are profoundly affected by memory. Content word substitutions are given in Table A.6.

Function Words.

Function words were commonly revised to fit a plausible interpretation of sentences. The most commonly affected function words were articles. In some contexts, a target *the* was as likely to be reported as *a* and vice versa. For example,

the parked truck → a parked truck
a cry in the night → the cry in the night.

In the same way, articles were omitted in appropriate contexts:

a chicken leg → chicken leg.

These errors were extremely numerous. Listeners seemed to supply articles almost automatically. A related extremely common error was

Death → ᴛʜɪs marks the end of our efforts.

TABLE A.6   Content Word Substitutions

Written response mode

Verb

glue → MOVE the sheep to the   background

lack → Smoky fires MAKE flame and heat

fires LET flame and heat

stunned → The beauty of the view STARTLED the young boy

hoist → PLACE the load to your left shoulder

mend → BUTTON the coat before you go out

MOVE the coat before you go out

ZIP the coat before you go out

cooked → was TIPPED before the bell rang

The meal was FINISHED before the bell rang

fool → The crooked maze failed to CONFUSE the mouse

bribed → He was FIRED because the new motor had to fail

He was FIRED because the new motor had failed

gnashed → The ape screamed and MASHED his yellow teeth (5×)

Subject

pint → A POT of tea helps to pass the evening (3×)

herring → Two blue HERON swam in the sink

purse → Her PULSE was full of useless trash

colt → The COLD reared and BLEW the sick rider

wrist → The RIP was badly straight and hung low

The ROAST was badly strained

The LIFT was badly strained and hung left

The ROOF was badly strained and hung

soup → This SHIRT tastes like stewed buzzard

gang → The friendly GAME is gone from the drug store (2×)

Object

rug → For quick cleaning, buy a BRUSH

For quick cleaning, buy a BROOM

depth → It's easy to tell the DUCK by the well

It's easy to tell the DUCK of a well

mouse → A perfect maze failed to fool the MAN

marrow → A cry in the night chills my HAIR

ducks → A dead dog is no use for hunting BIRDS

A dead dog is no use for a hunting DOG

(Continues)

TABLE A.6   (*Continued*)

coat → Mend the cook before you go out

flame → Smoky fires lack rain and heat

Object of preposition

view → The beauty of the rug stunned the young boy

sink → Two blue herring swam in the sea

        Two blue herring swam in the lake

reef → The ship was torn apart on the armory

        The ship was torn apart by the submarine

breach → Soldiers poured through the wide breaks in the wall

        Soldiers poured through the wide break in the wall (4×)

        Soldiers poured through the wide ridge in the wall

        Soldiers poured through the wide bridge in the wall

        Soldiers poured through the wide gap in the wall

buzzard → This soup tastes like stewed bugs (2×)

        This soup tastes like stewed onion

Modifier

blue → Two boiled   swam in the sink

green → The stray cat bore gray kittens (4×)

        The stray cat bore three kittens

        The stray cat had three kittens

        The stray cat   three kittens

coy → The quiet girl gave no clear response (2×)

        The quiet girl gave no response (2×)

crooked → The perfect maze failed to fool the mouse

Other

bribed → His bride caused the new motor to fail

read → we verse out loud for pleasure

ducks → A dead dog is no use for hunting now

        A dog is no use for protection

therein → We drank a coke with rum in it

wrist → The limb was badly strained and hung limp

limp → The wrist was badly strained and hung loose

Spoken response mode

Verb

glue → move the sheet in the dark blue background

        lose the sheet to the dark blue background

(*Continues*)

TABLE A.6   *(Continued)*

sue → FILL the bank under

grinned → The ape REAMED and gnashed his yellow teeth

        The ape CRANED and gnashed his yellowed teeth

cooked → The meal was FINISHED before the bell rang

thrown → The chest was STREWEN beside the parked truck

Subject

herring → Two blue HERONS swam

purse → The FIRST was full of youthful trash

      The FIRST was full of useful trash

wrist → The ROAST was badly strained and unlit

Object

disease → A pest may be a man or THIEF (2×)

heat → Smoky fires like flame and TEA

mouse → The crooked maid failed to fool the MAN (2×)

      The crooked maid failed to fool the NUN

coat → Mend the COOK before you go out

Modifier

useless → The first was full of YOUTH-full trash

green → The stray cat bore GRAY kittens

frosty → The GUSTY air passed through the coat

limp → The wrist was badly strained and hung LAP

Object of preposition

breach → Soldiers poured through the wide BREAK in the wall (5×)

      Soldiers poured through the wide CREASE in the wall

buzzard → This tastes like stewed BUGS

      This soup tastes like stewed ONION

living → What joy there is in MUDVILLE

      What joy there is in MONEY

ducks → A dead dog is no use for hunting DOGS

Just as content words sometimes were substituted by synonyms, function words were substituted by appropriate function words with a slightly different meaning. For example,

    beside → check was thrown BY the parked truck

        The chest was thrown INSIDE the parked truck

The chest was thrown BEHIND the parked truck
The chest was thrown ACROSS the parked crest.

All the substituted prepositions express a location or a direction, probably because it is required by the verb *thrown*. Substitutions for function words without radical restructuring of the target sentence are given in Table A.7.

Even though the listeners were participating in an experiment and had been told that they would be hearing grammatical though not necessarily perfectly appropriate sentences, they reported a few nonwords. These are given in Table A.8. Apparently, the phonological information available was simply not sufficient to enable listeners to find a word in the lexicon, yet it was specific enough to be reported.

Syntax

In the written response mode, there were a number of sentences which exhibited syntactic restructuring with varying degrees of accompanying phonological and lexical changes. Some erroneous reports of sentences seemed to result from one misidentified or miscategorized word. Other errors involved reporting the correct lexical items but in a different order, sometimes with and sometimes without accompanying changes in meaning. In still other cases, the basic structure of sentences was maintained but was filled with quite different lexical items. At the extreme, the relationship between the target sentence and the report was extremely distant.

Only two errors involve primarily word order. These are given in Table A.9. In one example, conjoined verbs were reported in a different order; in another, the word order appropriate for an exclamation was reordered to a declarative, with a change in meaning.

Errors in which an incorrect report of one word leads to changes in the syntactic form of a sentence are given in Table A.10. These errors also involved a change in the number of words reported, that is, in word boundary assignment. The most common error type was to report an unstressed syllable as a function word. Less often, a function word was added because the syntactic structure of the sentence required it. Content words were also supplied.

Syntactic errors which seem to occur because one word is misidentified or misclassified are given in Table A.11. In these errors, other changes, sometimes numerous, also occurred; that is, there were additions, deletions, or substitutions for portions of the target sentences. Nevertheless, the impression these reports leave is that one error places restrictions on possible continuations of a sentence and that these restrictions influence listeners' final reports.

Errors in which the relationship between the target and the reported sentence are more distant are given in Table A.12. These seem to be analogous to the extreme restructuring found for naturally occurring slips. At least in some

TABLE A.7 Errors Affecting Function Words

Written response mode

Verb form

is → It WAS easy to tell the depth of the well

was → check WITH

Prepositions

on → The ship was torn apart BY the sharp reef

depth → It's easy to tell the duck BY the well

to → blue sheet WITH a dart blue background

in the same → It snowed, rained, and hailed BY morning (2×)

beside → The chest was thrown INSIDE the parked truck

The chest was thrown BEHIND the parked truck

for → HER quick cleaning

HER quick (2×)

Other

death → THIS marks the end of our efforts (16×)

IT marks the end of our efforts

[word added] → smoothed UP planks

and → The ape grinned WITH in his teeth

our → the MORE effort

Spoken response mode

Prepositions

to → do the sheet WITH the dark blue background

beside → check was thrown BY the parked truck

The chest was thrown ACROSS the parked crest

to → Hoist the load OVER your left shoulder

on → The ship was torn apart BY the sharp reef (2×)

from → The friendly gang has gone TO the drug store

for → HER quick (2×)

HER quick   buy

Verb forms

to pass → A pint of tea HELPS pass the evening

is → The friendly gang HAS gone from the drug store

Other

it → IT'S snowed, rained, and hailed the same morning

TABLE A.8   Nonwords

<u>Written response mode</u>

coy → The ᴋᴏᴡ girl gave no green response

The ᴄᴏʀʏ girl gave no curious thoughts

mend → ᴀᴘ the coat before you go out

<u>Spoken response mode</u>

plunge → Hop over   ᴘᴜɴɢᴇ

groaned → The ape ɢʀᴀɴᴇᴅ and gnashed his yellow teeth

limp → The roast was badly strained and hung ʟᴏᴏɴ

false name → do the bank under ᴇxᴘᴜʟꜱɪɴᴀᴛɪᴏɴ

TABLE A.9   Errors in Word Order

<u>Written response mode</u>

What joy there is in living → What joy is there in living (2×)

It snowed, rained, and hailed the same morning → It rained, snowed, and hailed the same morning

<u>Spoken response mode</u>

It snowed, rained, and hailed the same morning → It snowed, hailed, and rained the same morning

cases, a rhythmic similarity between the target and the error is maintained. For example, there is a word for word substitution in the first part of the following two sentences:

Hop over the fence and plunge in →
Pop open the tank and plunge in
The meal was cooked before the bell rang →
Class was dismissed before the bell rang.

The syntactic structure and rhythmic pattern of the sentences were maintained.

Comparisons

The experimental errors and naturally occurring slips create the same overall impression, but they also exhibit some differences. The similarities seem to be the more significant. The distributions of error types was comparable. In the

TABLE A.10   Syntactic Errors Involve Change in Word Boundaries

---

Written response mode

Word added

Mesh wire keeps chickens inside → Mesh wire keeps chickens from flying (2×)

The coy girl gave no clear response → The boy and girl gave no response

He drank a Coke with rum therein → He drank a coke with rum and fizz

The crooked maze failed to fool the mouse → The cook at maze failed to fool the mouse

Rice is often served in round bowls → Bread crumbs are served in round bowls

Word lost

The hogs were fed chopped corn and garbage → The hogs looked at chopped corn and garbage

   The hogs prefer chopped corn and garbage

Spoken response mode

Word added

Mesh wire keeps chickens inside → Mesh wire keeps chickens from flying (2×)

Word lost

A cry in the night chills my marrow → A crying at night chills my marrow

   A cry at   shows my marrow

The colt reared and threw the sick rider → The colt reared and threw its rider

---

experimental reports, there were no stress errors and few vowel errors. Consonant errors involved substitutions as well as a few additions and deletions. The substitutions were errors of manner, place, and voicing, with a strong tendency for obstruents and resonants to be kept distinct. There were errors in syllable number and word boundary assignment as well as errors in function words and inflectional morphemes which could best be termed "editing." Finally, there were syntactic errors which maintained the overall rhythmic pattern of the targets with a great many detailed restructurings.

The differences resided primarily in the profound semantic and grammatical effects, such as reporting synonyms and maintaining syntactic structure. Many of these errors had little phonological support in the target sentences.

Explanations for these differences are not difficult to find. The experimental reports came from a limited number of speakers and listeners in a situation in which the listeners felt obligated to respond in some way. In contrast, natural slips were supplied voluntarily by a larger and more diverse population of speakers and listeners. The most noticeable difference between natural and experimental errors, the semantic effects, probably resulted from just this factor.

TABLE A.11 Syntactic Errors Involve Change in Word Function

Written response mode

Sue the bank under a false name →

Who robbed the bank under a false name

A dead dog is no use for hunting ducks →

A dead dog is no use for us now

The wrist was badly strained and hung limp →

The wrist was badly strained and broken

The voice was badly strained and bad

Smoky fires lack flame and heat →

A smoky fire's black flame and heat

Glue the sheet to the dark blue background →

Though the sheep to the dark

The colt reared and threw the sick rider →

The cold through the sick rider

The cult retired and threw the sick rider

Read verse out loud for pleasure →

Please first out loud for pleasure

We verse out loud for pleasure

He was bribed to cause the new motor to fail →

His bride caused the new motor to fail

He was fired because the new motor had to fail

He was bribed because the new motor had failed

He was fired because the new motor had failed because the new motor had failed

He was bribed the cause the new motor that failed

He was bribed, caused the new motor to fail caused the new motor to fail

He drank a Coke with rum therein →

Drink a Coke with rum therein

The crooked maze failed to fool the mouse →

The crooked maid failed to pull it off

The crooked maid failed to fold the map

Hoist the load to your left shoulder →

Voice the word to your left shoulder

The stray cat bore green kittens →

The stray cat wore green boots

The stray cat grew green kittens

(Continues)

TABLE A.11 *(Continued)*

Soldiers poured through the wide breach in the wall →

    Soldiers tore through the white reef to the wall

Spoken response mode

Smoky fires lack flame and heat →

    Smoky fires like flame and tea

He drank a Coke with rum therein →

    Drink a Coke with rum therein

Rice is often served in round bowls →

    The rice is cured in round bowls

The chest was thrown beside the parked truck →

    The chest was thrown across the parked crest

Soldiers poured through the wide breach in the wall →

    Soldiers tore through the white reef to the wall

Mesh wire keeps chickens inside →

    Mesh wire keeps chickens sighing

The colt reared and threw the sick rider →

    The cold vered through the sick rider

TABLE A.12 Syntactic Errors Showing Considerable Restructuring of the Target Sentence

Written response mode

Smoky fires lack flame and heat →

    Fires last flame in heat

A pest may be a man or a disease →

    Hence there be a man

    This be a man or his feet

The wrist was badly strained and hung limp →

    The road was badly frayed and unopen

The ape grinned and gnashed his yellow teeth →

    The ate cream and mottled his yellow teeth

    The ape ran and mashed the yellow key

    The man grasped and grit his teeth

(Continues)

TABLE A.12   (*Continued*)

The chest was thrown beside the parked truck →
   Check the phone by the parked truck
   Check the girl beside the parked car
   Check the road beside you park the truck
Glue the sheet to the dark blue background →
   Though the sheep to the dark
   Move the sheet to the drawer in the back
   Move the sheet of duck tape back there
   Move the sheep with the dreadful background
   Below the sheet there's dark blue background
A cry in the night chills my marrow →
   Flying at night
   Fay of night chills my marrow
Hop over the fence and plunge in →
   Part of the thing plunged in
   Fog came over the lake
   The set over near the sink needs plunging
These days a chicken leg is a rare dish →
   Deep-baked chicken is a rare dish
   Beef and chicken are like a rare dish
   These days chicks like
John is just a dope of long standing →
   John and Chuck are known
   John is just a dope with blonde skin
   John jumped over the long candle
For quick cleaning, buy a hemp rug →
   For cleaned five in a row
   The quick queen went by
An eel tastes sweet but looks awful →
   An eel   but worked often
The coy girl gave no clear response →
   The coy girl gave weary thoughts
The frosty air passed through the coat →
   The   through the pass past the coach
The meal was cooked before the bell rang →
   The meat was served before the bell rang
   split with fair women

(*Continues*)

TABLE A.12   *(Continued)*

What joy there is in living →
   What was the bridge in London
A king ruled the state in the early days →
   The king ruled the state and the other men
This soup tastes like stewed buzzard →
   Guess what he did now
The hum of bees made Jim sleepy →
   The hum of bees made Jim sleep easy
   With the help of these we just may beat
   The bees just may be lazy

Spoken response mode

A pest may be a man or a disease →
   A test may be a man or entity
Rice is often served in round bowls →
   Rice can not be served in round bowls
A pint of tea helps to pass the evening →
   Tom of tea helps to pass the evening
The hum of bees made Jim sleepy →
   Heavenly bees may be sleeping
Smoky fires lack flame and heat →
   The less he fires the less flame and heat
   Smoky fires left plane and heat
Glue the sheet to the dark blue background →
   Move the sheep to the background
   Two sheep were dark in the background
It's easy to tell the depth of a well →
   He could even tell the depth of a well
The colt reared and threw the sick rider →
   Cold beer entered the sick rider
John is just a dope of long standing →
   John and Chuck drove a long standing
   John just leaned over long standing
The meal was cooked before the bell rang →
   Class was dismissed before the bell rang
The wrist was badly strained and hung limp →
   The wrist was badly bent and limp

(Continues)

What joy there is in living →
   What was northern in inland
Hop over the fence and plunge in →
   Pop open the tank and plunge in
Sue the bank under a false name →
   Try the bank over the stream
It's easy to tell the depth of a well
   See if you can tell the depth of a well
   It was he who could tell the depth of the well
      Repeating well the depth so well
      Repeat down the depth of the well
Rice is often served in round bowls →
   Right or wrong it is not served in a brown bowl
   Write cross the word around the bone
   the surgeon Ralph Gold
   Craig did not deserve a round bowl
A pint of tea helps to pass the evening →
   The planet P helps to pass the E thing
   The planet V helps the pair beneath me
   The planet Z helps beneath me
   The pun in P helps to pass the evening
   A pint of pea helps to pass the ET
   The planet P helped

The similarities between the experimental errors and natural slips suggest that slips provide a window on the operation of speech perception and language-understanding systems and that data from slips are congruent with experimental data.

Data Set

Adults: Vowel Misperceptions

1. What's wrong with her bike? → her back

2. Wattsville → Whitesville (North Carolina to Ohio)

3. It really turned wet out → white out

4. It's like a math problem → mouth problem

5. Did I ever tell you about this usher? → this esher

6. where we went to the horse show → horse shoe

7. a lot of nude beaches → nude bitches

8. I don't know if we have any more "trecks" left → tracks left

9. You know that soil can be → swail can be

10. Fleischmann's → Flashman's

11. Flashman's → Fleshman's

12. color → collar

13. We'll get a house → will get a house

14. You're very fickle → very fecal

15. The bell isn't working → the bill

16. There are some cattle farmers → kettle farmers

17. That's a special → spatial

18. Vowels are a whole 'nother kettle of fish → cattle of fish

19. sheik-like → shake-like

20. stir this → store this

21. favorite kind of shirts → of shorts

22. Cherri and me → cheery and me

23. This blond guy in my class → blind guy

24. Swaney → Sweeney

25. kings → kangs

26. kings → cans

27. It's a chain tool → chine tool

28. Jan → Gene

29. Gene → Jan

30. Wendy will come → Windy

31. He's going to write a paper on tonology → on tenology

32. Pete Johnson → Jensen

33. Grammar Workshop → grandma workshop

34. Beowulf is received by Hrothgar in Heorot → by Hrothgar and Heorot

35. He's an ENT → an E and T

36. swimming and Greek → swimming in Greek

37. her system collapsed → her sister collapsed

38. I went nuts → I want nuts

39. The British have light l's → ales

40. Alan → Ellen

41. Verner → Verna

42. Some are better at → bitter

43. Are you barn members? → born members

44. I wanna catch Lloyd Rice → Lord Rice

45. Joe's going to → jaws going to

Adults: Consonant Misperceptions

46. a star who does not use a professional claque → professional clack

47. back to the grass roots → the grasp roots

48. ballistic conditions → felistic conditions

49. has been cool and collected → cruel and collected

50. having a nice van like that → nice man like that

51. it looks like it's carved of teak →teeth

52. porpoise lady → corpus lady

53. Curt → hurt

54. slip of the ear, *tlumbering* → *klumbering*

55. the article → the yarticle

56. the nodes of the moon → the nose

57. an afe → an eighth

58. and so has Stinziano → Tinziano

59. atmosphere → atnosphere

60. booty → boolie

61. chamelion → comedian

62. chicken poulette → chicken filet

63. contextual cues → contextual pews

64. cushion sole → kutchion sole

65. dialect divergence → dialect diversions

66. do you have a map of Mars → of bars

67. finger in your ear → in your rear

68. great → grape

69. greatest hits → greatest tits

70. geyser → Geiger

71. hey, man → hey, ma'am

72. hire some halls → some whores

73. honors, awards → otter's awards

74. insufficient → inefficient

75. Key lime pie → key line pie

76. L D B D → L D D D

77. little fritter → little critter

78. ma'am → pam

79. mag card → mad card

80. nasalization → navalization

81. parrot → carrot

82. phone → thone

83. professional claque → clap

84. remember chain rule → Jane Rule

85. sitter problems → sinter

86. sitting here for the last two hours snipping dates → sniffing dates

87. slip of the ear → snip of the ear

88. some rice → some ice

89. Do you have ice? → rice

90. studying Javanese internally → studying Javanese eternally

91. Terry Brazelton → Grazelton

92. the key to humility → to humidity

93. the Coke went flying → the coat went flying

94. too much air → too much hair

95. traitor → trader

96. trap → track

97. we need somebody with C's breathing in the building → breeding in the building

98. you are hearing Appalachian → hearing appellation

99. a basket of apples → amples

100. a poor house → a whore house

101. all of the members grew up in Philadelphia → threw up

102. Andy's going to fall asleep → Annie's

103. at least this part of it → this park of it

104. Bay Village → Faye Village

105. Benny Pate → Benny Bate

106. Bloomfield's personality was warped here → Whorfed here

107. Bob said it was noon → was nude

108. Bruce Galtter → Bruce Blatter

109. but next week I'll start using it pretty extensively → expensively

110. Captain Cook → Captain Hook

111. Chicago Witch Hunt → Chicago wish hunt

112. Councilman Portman → Cortman

113. Dad, have you ever heard of blueing? → of gluing

114. Dad's Fad → bad

115. *Death in Venice* → *Deaf in Venice*

116. Did you hear the guide in the Bishop White House? → the guy in the

117. Do you know what geodes are? → G O's

118. Does he come to class everyday? → Does she come to class

119. Don't forget the formula for the bridge cable → for the bridge table

120. Dr. Garber → Dr. Harber

121. Duke of Buckingham → Duke of Fuckingham

122. DC-9 → VC-9

123. Epley → Ekley

124. Fifth Street → fifth string

125. fine sunny weather → fine Sunday weather

126. Garnes → /dʒarnes/

127. Gary Dalton → very Dalton

128. Grape Nuts cereal → great nuts cereal

129. grape arbor → grate arbor [as in "grate cheese"]

130. Groton Court → Gloton Court

131. have her call Mike Rupright → Rutright

132. Have you seen Rod lately? → Ron lately

133. He hasn't heard of any viable reasons → buyable reasons

134. He is in the turkey-raising business → turkey-racing business

135. he must be a good Greek → good grief

136. he understands move → mood

137. He understands move → mooth

138. He's got a CB too → CV too

139. Her niece was in the hospital → her knees

140. Hi, Rob → Hi, Rod

141. house plants → house plans

142. How do you spell "savor"? → spell "sabre"

143. How do you spell "diverse"? → "divert"

144. How many moos did A. get? → moves did A. get?

145. Hulon Willis → Huron Willis

146. I can see you at four → I can't see you at four

147. I don't like her black hat on the floor → black cat on the floor

148. I gave him a lift today → a list today

149. I have to say good-bye to the Frys → flies

150. I just talked to her and saw Maria → Marina

151. I read Coomb's paper last night → Kuhn's paper

152. I saw a rusty old cart → car

153. I stayed home and made some drapes → made some grapes

154. I tell MBAs what to do → NBAs

155. I used to use that thing wrong → that thing long

156. I want to get a Coke → get a coat

157. I want to go out to Wilderness Trace and buy a cup → a cuff

158. I want to go see *Family Plot* → Family Klott

159. I wonder where Jimmy is going? → Timmy is going.

160. I'd like a Krackle → cracker

161. I'll bet that'll be a teary program → cheery program

162. I'm a phrenologist → phonologist

163. I'm getting married this Friday → buried this Friday

164. I'm trying to find some matches → some latches

165. if it wasn't a humid country → human country

166. in harmony with the text → test

167. It's D R O I N O → B R O I N O

168. It's going to be offered by Eastern → Easter

169. it's Lawson → Larson

170. Jim's out with his van → Jim's out with his fan

171. Joann Fokes → Cokes

172. *Kamasutra* → *Karmasutra*

173. Karen → Darren

174. Lasnik, Fiengo → Lasnik, Liengo

175. Lawnview → Longview

176. Lenny Willis returns the ball → Renny Willis

177. Long's → lawns

178. mouli → moody

179. mouli → moony

180. Move → moo

181. Mr. Hawbecker → Mr. Holbecker

182. Mr. Sands mother's neighbor → Mr. Sans

183. Mrs. Winner → Winter

184. My name is Goes, like walk → Ghost

185. Noam Chomsky leads a double life → double lie

186. Patwin → Pa?win

187. Romy is pregnant again → Robbie

188. She doesn't know what he's doing → know what she's doing

189. She had on a trench suit → a French suit

190. She writes comments on our papers → comets

191. She'll be home in about half an hour if I know her pace → her face

192. Scandinavian languages → Standinavian

193. slip of the ear → slip of the year

194. striking San Francisco doctors → dockers

195. stupid ship can't even survive a storm → stupid shit

196. Tagalog → thagalog

197. That's the wrong time → long time

198. the mining of Haiphong harbor → Haithong harbor

199. The only thing it doesn't work with for us is onions → bunions

200. the white sauce ladies → the white socks ladies

201. There's a car named the Roadrunner → the Roserunner

202. There's a word I learned in high school—*slovern* → *slobbern*

203. There's Jay → Where's Jay?

204. They can take cars to school → cards

205. They drop their g's → their jeans

206. They had a section for the deaf → for the death

207. They're all power people → our people

208. They're going to shoot trap → to shoot track

209. This picture does justice to Pei → Peg

210. train → tray

211. two twenty-eight → two twenty a

212. undramatical → ungrammatical

213. We start our summer league tonight → summer leave

214. We're going to go around and frenetically pick up the living room
    → phonetically pick up the living room

215. We're talking about the winter of '75 → winner

216. What are those sticks? → those ticks

217. What kind of pans did you use →pants

218. What's a corpus lady? → porpoise lady

219. When their condition → air condition

220. When were you in the service? → circus

221. When you were little did you wear a corset, Mom? → wear a corsep

222. Where's the cap? → the cat

223. Who → goo

224. Who? → oo

225. *Wie geht's* → i gates

226. Will the class → will the glass

227. Wilmington → Willington

228. Write the word "osill" → fossil

229. Yosemite → Dosemite

230. You can weld with it—braze → braids

231. You leave too much air in there → hair

232. You're a goon brain → a boon brain

233. an exam at Kent State → Wayne State

234. teaching summer quarter is worth two-ninths → is worth two nights

235. plain talk → play talk

236. training for great book → grade book

237. This is Six news at eight → This is Dick's news

238. face → mace

239. Do they have wigs → wings

240. Kim Adams → Tim Adams

241. Rudal → Rudolf

Adults: Complex Errors

242. Flum → mom

243. Eddie Hall → Betty Hall

244. this nation → the station

245. mail → mayo

246. IMSAI → INZAI

247. support services → sport services

248. sounds interesting → sounds intriguing

249. look at the cloud cover → card cover

250. pathology → psychology

251. Office of Public Occasions → Office of Publication

252. think about your valves → your vowels

253. I didn't know he had a big fancy car like that → big

254. I tripped on a tent pole → on a tadpole

255. Chris DePino → Christofino

256. vowels excerpted from "heed" words → key words

257. a bee flying backward → a beef lying backward

258. professional SAS programing secrets → professional essayist

259. a big heavy ring → a big heavy rain

260. Yoshimura → Yo Shimura

261. a diet to increase my sexual potency → to appease my sexual potency

262. a fancy seductive letter → a fancy structive letter

263. a fresh salad → a French salad

264. constraint-based phonology → straight-faced phonology

265. fresh artillery fire in Croatia → French artillery fire

266. red spire pears → red spider pears

267. and tell → until

268. a linguini is a noodle → a lean Wheatie is a noodle

269. a little wine → a little lime

270. Thai food → taiphoon

271. a loose end in this problem → a leaf's end

272. a phonetic explanation of phonology by Ohala → by Halle

273. a process of residence selection → residence lection

274. a purse and a billfold → a personal billfold

275. a slant board → a sled board

276. a small computer → a smoke computer

277. a very exotic child → erotic child

278. a Bulova watch → Bova watch

279. a U-Haul in front of us → an ink ball in front of us

280. about some follow-up → some foul-up

281. accidents → actions

282. an apartment for a hundred and ten a month → for ten a month

283. an errand to run near High Street → to run on New High Street

284. an honors political science course → honest political science course

285. an imitative → an inervative

286. and this function word, by → function verb

287. assigned to the grad coordinator → grant coordinator

288. assorted → a sordid

289. I've been doing research → a search

290. Kate O'Berin → Kato Berin

291. at the parasession → at the Paris session

292. attacks in the ear → a tax on the ear

293. back window → tack one doe

294. barrel → bottle

295. boiled these pearls in cherry preserves → in chili preserves

296. book on primate infants → primate incest

297. bookshop → bookshelf

298. Avalanche → evelinsh [in context of hockey player Ozolinsh]

299. boustraphedic → posturpedic

300. bubonic → Blue Bonnet

301. catch a five-pounder → catch a flounder

302. cathedral → gazebo

303. change for a dollar → exchange a dollar

304. choose any nineteen → two seventy nineteen

305. cinema and photography → cinnamon photography

306. citrus craving → citrus gravy

307. cloudy → ploddy

308. conditions are almost right → Hendersons are almost right

309. converge en masse → conversion mass

310. cracked → track

311. Dec man tomorrow? → Pacman tomorrow

312. Did you see my Nancy Reagan cards? → ANSI rating cards

313. Dix Ward → Dick Sward

314. Do you have any aspirin? → Do you have a napkin

315. eat a Maple Leaf wiener → a make-believe wiener

316. erudite → area dried

317. everybody's human → everybody's showman

318. evolution of tense systems → of intense systems

319. falling tone → foreign tone

320. felicity conditions → ballistic conditions

321. foods → fruits

322. found a copy → pound of coffee

323. four to five weeks → forty-five weeks

324. four wheat pennies → four weekends

325. foxglove → fox globe

326. foxglove → fox glow

327. from 180 some → for 180 some

328. frothing → throfing

329. fruits and vegetables → prudent vegetables

330. gallons and gallons of coffee → jallons and jallons

331. get me a mine → get me some wine

332. get my other cookbooks → my etiquette books

333. get your ducks in a row → get your guts in a row

334. giving an award → giving an oral

335. glottal wave of the deaf → auto wave of the deaf

336. go to a party → to a burly

337. got a reaction → gonorrhea action

338. grant → camp

339. he and Annie's father → he and his father

340. heart to heart → hard to hard

341. her fiancé's Canadian → comedian

342. her system collapsed → her sister

343. hero sandwich → harrah sandwich

344. hockey pucks → coffee pots

345. hypnotic age regression → hypnotic aid to regression

346. I have a weed trimmer → weak tremor

347. I know what happened to our ice, Andy → to high Sandy

348. I need to talk to him → I need to calculate

349. illegible → illogical

350. imagery → energy

351. important → imported

352. in different positions → indifferent physicians

353. inflection → inflation

354. instruction class → destruction class

355. interestin' → Enarson

356. interview → ennerview

357. it costs six to seven dollars to replace → sixty-seven dollars

358. it would hurt it → it would pervert it

359. just bisecting lines → just bicycling

360. kills germs where they grow → kills germs with egg roll

361. lawn chair → launcher

362. lighter → ladder

363. lingonberries → lindenberries

364. living with a coach → women who coach

365. loan word → long word

366. low visibility → lovas

367. lunch in a huge cafeteria → in a Jewish cafeteria

368. Mary, would you like some tea with this? → like to eat with us?

369. matches → mattress

370. meaningfulness → mean influence

371. meet Mr. Anderson → Mr. Edison

372. mental science → middle science

373. meteor → meat eater

374. missed the news → must a snoozed

375. movement → Newton

376. my appointment was rather long → running long

377. my coffee cup refilled → my coffee cup fell

378. my three-ninety class → my three-D night class

379. myo-functional therapy → mild functional therapy

380. name is being withheld → repelled

381. neatest → meanest

382. no bullshit exams → noble shit exams

383. no, she isn't → no shitting

384. No shit, Little Beaver → no shittling beaver

385. nonaccessible storage → nonaggressible storage

386. notary public → Nota republic

387. off → up

388. on an island with a moat surrounding it → with moats surrounding it

389. on neurolinguistics → on zero linguistics

390. on the middle staircase → the mill staircase

391. one cup of weak coffee → one Cocoa Wheat Puff

392. one of the court poets → the poor poets

393. orgasm → organism

394. "osill" → asshole

395. overcorrection → overt correction

396. parachute → pair of shoes

397. passed with a four → with a full

398. Paula played with Tom → polyp-laden θam

399. plant dying → plant dung

400. portrait → poetry [speaker is British]

401. "precise-ities" → precise cities

402. psychic → psychotic

403. pull course → cool course

404. quiet → buy it

405. raised chocolate donut → glazed chocolate

406. repairing foreign cars → falling cars

407. roll up the back window → patroll the back window

408. round trip → one trip

409. rural free delivery → oral free delivery

410. savor → sable

411. seismology → psychology

412. setting up of time → studying of time

413. sewing it → selling it

414. shabby furniture → Chevy

415. furniture she wants to be a teacher → she wants me to teach her

416. she's ripe → she's raped

417. someone else isn't neat this morning → is in heat this morning

418. something like *Poseidon Adventure* → like a silent adventure

419. speech science → speech sinus spun

420. toffee → fun stocking

421. Star Fire → /sta fa/

422. still lousy → still assy

423. structure, style, and usage → instruct your style and usage

424. tendency → Tennessee

425. the anechoic chamber → the ambionic chamber

426. the beings on Mars have destroyed our latest spececraft → the beans

427. the Clemency Information Center → the Columbus Information Center

428. the Codofil people → the colorful people

429. the floor of the House → the Florida house

430. the habitat → the havercamp

431. the holy book → phoney book

432. the meaning of the word average has changed over the years → the mean of the average

433. the most literate → most illiterate

434. the O.E.D → D.O.E.D.

435. the Old Creek Inn was deserted → creek end was deserted

436. the paramour → the power mower

437. the pony league → pointer league

438. the radio on → the regular one

439. the Arabs and the Israelis → herbs and the Israelis

440. *The Ascent of Man* → the scent of man

441. the *Edmond Fitzgerald* → Edna Fitzgerald

442. the P O N → the P L N

443. It's there up ahead → It's clear up ahead

444. they took footprints when you were born → they took footprints in the dorm

445. they're all nuts → all nice

446. this heat → his heat

447. those shoes → oh, shoot

448. to go for Mike → Nicole for Mike

449. toast and jelly → toast and chili

450. too close to melt → to mouth

451. trained at Cornell → chained at Cornell

452. trying to get over being chairman → being German

453. two hundred hours → two hundred dollars

454. two models of speech perception → two miles

455. urination → you're a nation

456. usual grace period → illegal grace period

457. we had a representative of the preschool come → of the Peace Corps

458. we offered six → we Alfred six

459. white → quiet

460. white roll → rye roll

461. whose → goose

462. why I turned to Krylon → turned to crime

463. with drugs → at stud

464. without your mother along → without your mother-in-law

465. worse 'n that → where's Annette

466. wrapping service → wrecking service

467. your ladder → your letter

468. your nation → urination

469. A friend of ours is having a lung removed → is having alumni move

470. A lot of kids are going to Oswego → to Sweden

471. A H A → A A J

472. barbell set → bord la sell

473. Acton Road → Atkin Road

474. All she had was a glass of Dubonnet → of bubonic

475. Americana → a Mary Canna

476. Ann was afraid to go → afraid to do it

477. Anne Schwarz → had on shorts

478. Anybody see a tong → a comb

479. Anyone who thinks carob bean is a good substitute for chocolate is crazy → paraffin is a good substitute

480. Astrid Gilberto → bastard Gilberto

481. AFIT /æfɪt/ → effort

482. Bette Midler → Pat Miller

483. Bikerton → Pinkerton

484. Blair → Ware

485. Bruce is going to sing → Ruth

486. Bruce Galtter → Bruce Bladder

487. Can I saw? → crawl

488. Cathy needs change for the laundry → for the lottery

489. Chris Evert at Wimbledon → Prince Edward

490. Christy Bridge → Christy Grinch

491. Clara W I E C K → W I Z K

492. Claude → Rod

493. Coke and a Danish → coconut Danish

494. Couldn't you say that was an S P C? → was misperceived?

495. Debbie is fifth → is first

496. Dec writer → decorator

497. Dennis Molfesse brought all his students → Dennis Smallpiece

498. Dennison → dentist

499. Did you put the food out for him? → for them

500. Do you have any pith balls → any pit falls

501. Do you have any Wite-Out? → white album

502. Do you know anything about four-term analogy? → about four terminology

503. Do you know new dimensions → know nude mentions

504. Do you know a Greg Cortina → Do you own

505. Do you want me to recite? → to recycle

506. Does he have any hair? → any higher

507. Don't make it a horse story → a horror story

508. Don't you think it's a lot like punk → like pump

509. Dover sole → Dover salad

510. Dr. Dierker → Dr. Diargood

511. Ed McMahon → ethnic man

512. Everything's about a quarter more → about a quart or more

513. Exotic birds from far-off lands are fascinating → are assassinating

514. Falstaff → Flagstaff

515. Father Joe and → Father Joan

516. Finn → friend

517. First stop of his four-nation tour → phonation tour

518. Five-sixths of all conversions in the church → of all conversations

519. In four to six months we'll get a house → four to six marks will get you a house

520. Front vowels occur only in words → Front vowels are Kyrolean *words*

521. Garnes → Garmens

522. Geez, really? → Disraeli

523. German's looking for a room → Jim's looking

524. Get a pill out → a pillow

525. Givon → pavane

526. Good old zebra's law → zebra slaw

527. Greektown → Wheattown

528. Haggai's thesis → the guy's thesis

529. He could run his son → burn his son

530. He doesn't mow his own lawn → He doesn't blow his own horn

531. He got ten years in prison → tenure in prison

532. He runs a driving school → a drive-in school

533. He works in an herb and spice shop → an urban spice shop

534. He's a fiscal liberal → physical liberal

535. He's out supervising the back hoe → supervising tobacco

536. He's Snoopy in disguise → in the skies

537. Hello, big boy → big Bart

538. Herbert H. Lehman College → Heritage Lehman College

539. Hi, Cupid → hi, Cuban

540. Hi-C → ice tea

541. His name is Swain → Swaney

542. How about your tires? → your title

543. How do you spell "Cochran" → spell popcorn

544. How does the west look? → the bus look

545. How's your work going? → book going

546. How's David? → How's Gregg?

547. Hyman → Lehmann

548. I already claimed it → cleaned it

549. I am a wombat → a woman

550. I bought a slide hammer → slide camera

551. I called Tarpy's → Karki's

552. I can ink it in → can nick it in

553. I didn't have to wear a coat → to work

554. I don't fight for causes → find for causes

555. I don't intend to stay in the picture → to stain the picture

556. I don't think of the bass as a solo instrument → as so low an
     instrument

557. I don't think we could afford to bring him here → could get a Ford
     to bring him here

558. I feel secure → I disappear

559. I found it → Icelandic

560. I get to leave this place → I can't believe this place

561. I got to sleep at a decent hour → to sleep at least an hour

562. I have a dental appointment → a dinner appointment

563. I have them do out-of-class writing → auto class writing

564. I have to eat, too → I have eighty-two

565. I have to go to the moon at six → to the mint at six

566. I just got back from Denison → back from dentist

567. I just like it → I dislike it

568. I kept an eye on the Big Dipper last night → I kept denying the Big *Dipper*

569. I know where she can get really young kids → dumb kids

570. I know where the place is → what the place is

571. I love you and my baby → I love you. You are my baby

572. I need a loose crew → loose screw

573. I need air → I need earmuffs

574. I say crayon → crown

575. I scream → ice cream

576. I take a couple of Anacin → a cup of acid

577. I teach speech science → speech signs

578. I think it's a penguin → a pink one

579. I think I see a place → I think I see his face

580. I want to go out to a state park → to a steak bar

581. I was running around after a slide projector → after a sniper

582. I was through on a bus → I was thrown off a bus

583. I wouldn't eat at the restaurant in a motel unless it's snowing → unless it's smelly

584. I'll catch my breath here → catch my breakfast

585. I'll catch my breath here → my brushup

586. I'm conking out → coffee out

587. I'm covered with chalk dust → with chocolate

588. I'm going to try to get it towed → to get a toad

589. I'm going up for my office hours → for my vodka sours

590. I'm going with the Dean → with the team

591. I'm horny → it's morning

592. I'm in the Political Science Department → pickle science department

593. I'm making boats → taking notes

594. I'm not American → not a miracle

595. I'm on a trip now → a chip one

596. I'm serious → I'm furious

597. I'm staying near O'Hare → more O'Hare

598. I've never cooked anybody's goose → cooked anybody mousse

599. Is he nasty? → Is he an ass?

600. Is that home baked? → Is that hard to bake?

601. Is that margarine? → Is that Mondrian?

602. Isn't this nice for a border? → a quarter

603. It depends on the fins → on the spin

604. It will be a tenting situation → tempting situation

605. It will be done next year → in six years

606. It will be how many years? → It will be twenty years

607. It'll be a confusing weekend → You're confusing weekends

608. It's a dollar a quarter → It's a dollar and a quarter

609. It's always too short → always *toujours*

610. It's called *The Absence of a Cello* → *The Absence of Othello*

611. It's going to ring in a minute → rain in a minute

612. It's in a real forest → a real farce

613. It's made with ham bone → with hand bone

614. It's that lousy atomic bread I can't stand → Italian bread

615. It's typed → his type

616. IREX /aireks/ → I was

617. Jakarta → Chicago [British speaker]

618. Jane Kollaritsch → Jane Clark

619. Jean and I → Gina [unclear last name]

620. Jefferson Starship → Jeffers and starship

621. John Eulenberg → John Gilbert

622. Latvian festival → Latvian Eskimo

623. Leena → Elena

624. Legg and Davis → Leggett Davis

625. Let me now try to develop this point → not try to develop

626. Levi Jackson → Levi Jetson

627. Lisa has good taste → she has good taste

628. Louisiana → New Zealand

629. for all intents and purposes → for all intensive purposes

630. Mad River Township → Madrigal Township

631. Mandarin Chinese food → Mandarin Chinese flu

632. Many a father has been greeted by a roller skate → created by a roller skate

633. Mar Dee Doll → Marty Dow

634. Maybe we ought to give up descriptive linguistics → give up the script of linguistics

635. Mom, he did it → Mommy did it

636. Mrs. Herrell → Mrs. Hill

637. My handout isn't as good as I hoped it would be → I told it would be

638. Nelson → Neusa

639. Noel Matkin → Noam Atkin

640. Olga's son → the sun

641. Orrin W. Robinson → R. N. W. Robinson

642. P E O → B O

643. Pat Miller → Jack Miller

644. Penn State → Kent State

645. Pier One Imports → beer wine imports

646. Room 260 is locked → is a lot

647. RP-ized → R P I

648. Sara → sir

649. Sara Garnes and Ilse → Sara Garnes Nielsen

650. See the giant meadow muffin → metal muffin

651. She lives in that same area → saint area

652. She's working for the Judiciary Committee → Jewish charity committee

653. Siever's law → zebra's law

654. Skippers' treat → trick or treat

655. So you're going to be there two years in a row? → to be edder two years

656. Sometimes it's a woman → running

657. Southern California → Summit California

658. SUNOCO has a battery → snorkel has a battery

659. SWAT leader → swamp leaper

660. 't shows → Joe's

661. Texas Women's University → Texas Lumens University

662. That's a good idea for the future → What's a good idea

663. That's a good way to get your car door taken off → your carburator taken off

664. That's an *L* → an A–O

665. That's not a part of the remedial program → the reading program

666. That's the kind he used before → used in the Air Force

667. The book I would recommend is by Paul Zemmlin → Zemler

668. The bottom's all covered with eels → the bob

669. The king spoke in a flawed style → florid style

670. The report is tolerable → is horrible

671. The urn is finished → the urine is finished

672. There's some iced tea made → there's a nice teammate

673. They had a ten-year party → a tenure party

674. They must be members of the Republican party → of the Republic of Hardy

675. They're all Appalachian whites → Appalachian waste

676. They're getting off their course → their chorus

677. This Acoustical Society → the Sacoustical Society

678. This friend of ours who visited → of ours is an idiot

679. This goes through forty-eight → through Fourier

680. This is mystery dressing → Mr. Dressing

681. This kid was afraid of rapids → of rabbits

682. Those are nice pants → nice peanuts

683. Trudy → tree

684. Try newspaper and a hot iron → hot air

685. Viennese → Vietnamese

686. Wardhaugh → warthog

687. Wardhaugh → Wardhol

688. We are going to buy a new bed → new vet

689. We are moving seven calves → seven cats

690. We are not using the accident rates yet → not using the accident rate shit

691. We could give them an ice bucket → a nice bucket

692. We eat at eight → we needed eight

693. We got our task force grant → our tennis court grant

694. We had this appointment . . . → disappointment

695. We must get some sealing tape → ceiling paint

696. We were in Amherst together → enamorous together

697. We will just arrest him → molest him

698. We're going to pour him into the car → Purim into the car

699. We're going to stay in Tebins → in tenements

700. We're going to Xenia → to Adena

701. Well, I'll sit here and peck away some more → decolate some more

702. Westover → Westoak

703. stomach flu → summit flu

704. doggie → donkey

705. representational → reputational

706. What does *vivace* /vivəs/ mean? → *bibas*

707. What Phil Morse is going to do → what Fillmore is going to do

708. What's another word for *menorah* → for *manure*

709. casual informal → casual and formal

710. When were you here? → Why were

711. Who's calling? → Who's Colleen?

712. With less than two weeks to go → less than two weeks ago

713. Wouldn't she look good with a ring in her nose → oregano nose

714. You can spend a mint eating → you can spend a minute

715. You swallowed a watermelon → You smiled at a watermelon

716. You're not wearing one → not married

717. You've got all the books you need for the time being → for your typing

718. Your etiquette books → other cookbooks

719. nose and eyes → Molson Ice

720. wrangler → regular

721. Janet Jackson → Chada Jackson

722. He was in a wreck → in Iraq

723. Sonic, the hedgehog → son of the hedgehog

724. Do mountain lions have manes? → names

725. East Knox Local Schools → These Knox Local Schools

726. Riga → Eureka

727. attorney Larry L. Rowe → a dirty Larry L. Rowe

728. enshrinees' dinner → Chinese dinner

729. Harms → Harlens

730. West State Street → West Eighth Street

731. I lighted → I like it

Adults: Extensive Mismatch Between Utterance and Perception

732. Do you want a grape? → a drink

733. Old Navy store → oak baby store

734. making Polish pisanki → Polish prosody

735. a red jacket → a red cap

736. therapeutic hibachi → computer hibachi

737. they were going to Akron → to Africa

738. What's happening? → What's that mean?

739. a ride with Dr. von Gierke → in a Brown Derby

740. four wheat pennies → four weekends

741. Parcheesi set → Parmesan cheese

742. Friar Tuck pizza → Kentucky Fried pizza

743. typewriter → card table

744. After the rubber boat had been wrecked in the squall → After the rubber boot had been erected in the squirrel

745. You could light a small house with him → reminds you of Householder

746. *College Outline Grammar of French* → how to jabber in French

747. I read three articles and that's about it → I read three articles on phonetics

748. Are you going to have a baby? → Are you going out with David?

749. energy from the sun → hemorrhaging from the side

750. I didn't think he would let us use his car → I didn't think he'd last through the day

751. fixing sausage → fish sticks

752. discussions before tomorrow → discussions of Borg-Warner

753. Sorry kid, but you're not mine → It's your kid, not mine

754. Oh, *The Great Escape* → Oh, Fred Astaire

755. How've you been? → Got a minute?

756. I wasn't getting anywhere with all those vowel adjustments → with all those bottles of aspirin

757. I seem to be thirsty → I sing through my green Thursday

758. I have a headache → I haven't had any

759. prove some statement of Scriptures → prove some structural descriptions

760. I'm going to go back to bed until the news → I'm going to go back to bed and crush the noodles

761. pecan log → common law

762. Athens → Akron

763. I'm gonna try and get home before it rains → I'm gonna try to get hold of Fort Wayne

764. What else? → mayonnaise

765. I need to talk to him → need to calculate

766. bear country → Erica

767. That's the mother in me → that's the multirunway

768. Did you check the roast duck? → something was froze stuck

769. A linguini is a noodle → a lean Wheatie is a noodle

770. never enough → mother him up

771. the guy was there with the Indian cigarettes → the guy ordered VD and cigarettes

772. teach someone to act → do you know a rat

773. what the difference in the Bedouin case is → in the better one is

774. Orange Julius → on through no and yes

775. Art Garfunkel → our current fumble

776. John's nose is on crooked → John knows his own cooking

777. and your next appearance will be at Santa Laura College → as a saddle or a carriage

778. You sure like your booze → You don't like your boots

779. What's happening? → seven

780. It's happy Hudy time → It's *Howdy Doody* time

781. clash of the Titans → or else they're fighting

782. ceramics → *saimnieks* [Latvian, "farmer," a cross-linguistic misperception]

783. farmer-financier → thin man here

784. I'm gonna go home and work on my income tax → mop and wax

                    *   *   *

Children: Vowel Errors

 1. cuff him → cough him

 2. They have *s*'s up there → asses

 3. We'll pick you up Saturday → will pick you up

 4. a little pillbox → peel box

 5. You are supposed to put "a" or "an" before the words → /n/

 6. It's the Robin Hood principle → rabin (/æ/) Hood

 7. How do you spell "since"? → spell "sense"

 8. enchilada → anchilada

 9. Got milk? gut milk

Children: Consonant Errors

 10. bury → marry

11. chine tool → chime tool

12. chip in a dollar → hip in

13. chivaree [shivaree] → chivalry

14. comics → comets

15. her obituary → her habituary

16. home of the most famous ships that ply the seas → that fly the seas

17. lots of laminated wood → animated wood

18. molie → movie

19. pedal to the metal → to the medal

20. she landed in a hole → pole

21. that's a phi → a thigh

22. the acts of God → The ax of God

23. usher → husher

24. vampire → rampire

25. vase → face

26. Did you see the horse? It was spotted all over. → splotted all over

27. Do you have a nibble? → Do you have a nipple?

28. Do you know what *taksi* means in Finnish? → what *tapsy* means in Finnish

29. Do you want a coat? → a Coke

30. Family Klott → *Family Plot*

31. Hold → cold

32. How do you spell "savor"? → spell safer

33. I believe in Malcolm → in malko

34. I got it at the Tall Shop → doll shop

35. I put it in my book bag → in my book back

36. I think they're going to do the warts first → the wards

37. I wonder if they thought the windows were thermopanes → thermotanes

38. I'm not going to Dayton tomorrow → Payton tomorrow

39. *Je ne sais pas* → *Je ne sais ba* [English speakers]

40. Kon → Hon

41. Let's look for the cape → the cake

42. Letty Cooper → Betty Cooper

43. Look at this dirt → this girt

44. Mr. Hawbecker → Mr. Hawdecker

45. Mrs. High → Mrs. Pie

46. Obstetrician → obsetrician

47. That's no trick → no trip

48. That's ungrammatical speech → undramatical speech

49. The Big Leaguer → The Big Leader

50. The FDIC is here on the right → FBIC

51. There are some signs of an old mine → a gold mine

52. They held a sheet up in front of the married couple → held a sheep

53. They're getting off their course, you know → off their horse

54. This root → this Brut

55. Well, how about a plosive? → a klosive

56. What's a CV? → CB

57. Would you get the coats? → Cokes

58. the warts first → wards first

59. a matter of trial and error → trial and air

60. a rail to hang our lap robes on → our life robes on

61. book dump → mik dump

62. cigarettes → skrits

63. general → janitor

64. initial → official

65. ketchup → a chip

66. one of us will be very sorry → very sour

67. some bingo markers → bingle markers

68. the early administrations → menstrations

69. three-handed gin → three hundred gin

70. to missions → temissions

71. triangular → try angular

72. wax → glass

73. we'll have to coordinate → have a quarter to eight

74. what the song "Half-breed" is all about → song "half-free"

75. Are you from Holland? → from pollen

76. Asbjorn Olafson Vinje → Asjorn Olaf Vinje

77. Biting dogs and crowing hens → curling hens

78. Don't mix up the code of the road → Don't make zip the code

79. Feel this—it's cool → feel this at school

80. Grandfather had a new lap robe → Afro

81. He pretended he didn't know what a pair of skis were → where a pair of skis were

82. How many miles is Hawaii from the mainland → from Dominion

83. I told him to go and find the store → infine the store

84. I visited two classes today → missed two classes

85. I was looking at this photograph → this soda graph

86. I'm feeling more cheery → more scarry

87. I'm going to Miami → my yami

88. If you enjoyed Vietnam → enjoyed meat an' ham

89. Iowa's colors → iris colors

90. Isn't it nice not to have all these deadlines → all these dandelions

91. Mayor McCheese → American cheese

92. Mayor McCheese → Mayor get cheese

93. *Poor Richard's Almanac* is full of homey advice → phony advice

94. That's a good local program → loco program

95. The men are out lumbering in the forests → are out tlumbering

96. There are stars and → Tarzan

97. We're going on the Horace Mann Run → horse man run

98. What kind is it? → What time is it?

99. What kind of accent do you think that was? → what kind of exit

100. Where are your jeans? → Wear your jeans

101. Where did you get your tallness from? → your tongs from

102. Would you like to be a maid? → be amayd

103. They are on late → on a lake

104. Your eyes are kind of bloodshot → kind of blushing

105. She has green eyes → three eyes

106. Fifty-six G's → jeans

REFERENCES

Aitchinson, J. (1972). Mini-malapropisms. *British Journal of Disorders of Communication, 7,* 38–43.

Aitchison, J. (1987). *Words in the mind.* Oxford, UK: Blackwell.

Baayen, R. H. (1994). Productivity in language production. In D. Sandra & M. Taft (Eds.), *Morphological structure, lexical representation and lexical access* (pp. 447–469). Hillsdale, NJ: Lawrence Erlbaum Associates.

Bever, T. G., Lackner, J. R., & Kirk, R. (1969). The underlying structures of sentences are the primary units of immediate speech processing. *Perception and Psychophysics, 5,* 225–234.

Bond, Z. S. (1973). Perceptual errors in ordinary speech. *Zeitschrift für Phonetik, 26,* 691–695.

Bond, Z. S. (1976a). Identification of vowels excerpted from neutral and nasal contexts. *Journal of the Acoustical Society of America, 59,* 1229–1232.

Bond, Z. S. (1976b). Identification of vowels excerpted from /l/ and /r/ contexts. *Journal of the Acoustical Society of America, 60,* 906–910.

Bond, Z. S. (1981). Listening to elliptic speech: Pay attention to stressed vowels. *Journal of Phonetics, 9,* 89–96.

Bond, Z. S., & Garnes, S. (1980a). Misperceptions of fluent speech. In R. A. Cole (Ed.), *Perception and production of fluent speech* (pp. 115–132). Hillsdale, NJ: Lawrence Erlbaum Associates.

Bond, Z. S., & Garnes, S. (1980b). A slip of the ear: A snip of the ear? A slip of the year? In V. Fromkin (Ed.), *Errors in linguistic performance: Slips of the tongue, ear, pen and hand* (pp. 231–239). New York: Academic Press.

Bond, Z. S., Moore, T. J., & Gable, B. (1996). Listening in a second language. *Proceedings of the international conference on spoken language processing* (pp. 2151–2154). Philadelphia.

Bond, Z. S., & Robey, R. R. (1983). The phonetic structure of errors in the perception of fluent speech. In Norman J. Lass (Ed.), *Speech and language: Advances in basic research and practice* (pp. 249–283). New York: Academic Press.

Bond, Z. S., & Small, L. H. (1983). Voicing, vowel, and stress mispronunciations in continuous speech. *Perception and Psychophysics, 34,* 470–474.

Browman, C. (1980). Perceptual processing: Evidence from slips of the ear. In V. A. Fromkin (Ed.), *Errors of linguistic performance: Slips of the tongue, ear, pen, and hand* (pp. 213–230). New York: Aca-demic Press.

Brown, R., & McNeill, D. (1966). The "tip of the tongue" phenomenon. *Journal of Verbal Learning and Verbal Behavior, 8,* 325–337.

Butterfield, S., & Cutler, A. (1988). Segmentation errors by human listeners: Evidence for a prosodic segmentation strategy. *Proceedings of speech '88* (pp. 827–833). Edinburgh.

Celce-Murcia, M. (1980). On Meringer's corpus of "slips of the ear." In V. A. Fromkin (Ed.), *Errors of linguistic performance: Slips of the tongue, ear, pen, and hand* (pp. 199–211). New York: Academic Press.

Chaney, C. (1989). I pledge a legiance tothe flag: Three studies in word segmentation. *Applied Psycholinguistics, 10,* 261–281.

Chomsky, N. (1996). Language and thought. In *Powers and prospects: Reflections on human nature and the social order* (pp. 1–30). Boston: South End Press.

Cutler, A. (1986). Phonological structure in speech recognition. *Phonology Yearbook, 3,* 161–178.

Cutler, A., & Butterfield, S. (1992). Rhythmic cues to speech segmentation: Evidence from juncture misperception. *Journal of Memory and Language, 31,* 218–236.

Cutler, A., Mehler, J., Norris, D. & Segui, J. (1989). Limits on bilingualism. *Nature, 340,* 229–230.

Cutler, A., & Norris, D. (1988). The role of strong syllables in segmentation for lexical access. *Journal of Experimental Psychology: Human Perception and Performance, 14,* 113–121.

Dalby, J., Laver, J., & Hiller, S. M. (1986). Mid-class phonetic analysis for a continuous speech recognition system. *Proceedings of the Institute of Acoustics, 8,* 347–354.

Donegan, P. J., & Stampe, D. (1979). The study of natural phonology. In D. A. Dinsen (Ed.), *Current approaches to phonological theory* (pp. 126–173). Bloomington: Indiana University Press.

Egan, J. P. (1944). Articulation testing methods II. Office of Scientific Research and Development, Washington D.C., Report No. 3802.

Feldman, L. B., & Fowler, C. A. (1987). The inflected noun system in Serbo-Croatian: Lexical representation of morphological structure. *Memory and Cognition, 15,* 1–12.

Fodor, J. A., & Bever, T. (1965). The psychological reality of linguistic segments. *Journal of Verbal Learning and Verbal Behavior, 4,* 414–420.

Fodor, J. A., Garrett, M., & Bever, T. (1968). Some syntactic determinants of sentential complexity: II. Verb structure. *Perception and Psychophysics, 3,* 453–461.

Fokes, J., & Bond, Z. S. (1989). The vowels of stressed and unstressed syllables in non-native English. *Language Learning, 39,* 341–373.

Fokes, J., & Bond, Z. S. (1993). The elusive/illusive syllable. *Phonetica, 50,* 102–123.

Forster, K. I. (1976). Accessing the mental lexicon. In R. J. Wales & E. Walker (Eds.), *New approaches to a language mechanisms* (pp. 257–287). Amsterdam: North-Holland Publishers.

Garnes, S., & Bond, Z. S. (1975). Slips of the ear: Errors in perception of casual speech. *Procedings of the eleventh regional meeting of the Chicago Linguistic society* (pp. 214–225).

Gorrell, P. (1991). Subcategorization and sentence processing. In R. C. Berwick, S. P. Abney, & C. Tenny (Eds.), *Principle-based parsing: Computation and psycholinguistics* (pp. 279–300). Dordrecht, The Netherlands: Kluwer Academic Publishers.

Grosjean, F. (1980). Spoken word recognition and the gating paradigm. *Perception and psychophysics, 28,* 267–283.

Grosjean, F., & Gee, J. P. (1987). Prosodic structure and spoken word recognition. *Cognition, 25,* 135–155.

Hockett, C. F. (1973). Where the tongue slips, there slip I. In V. A. Fromkin (Ed.), The *Speech errors as linguistic evidence* (pp. 93–119). The Hague: Mouton. Reprinted from *To Honor Roman Jakobson,* The Hauge: Mouton, 1967.

Hockett, C. F. (1987). *Refurbishing our foundations: Elementary linguistics from an advanced point of view.* Amsterdam: John Benjamins.

Hood, J. D., & Poole, J. P. (1980). Influence of the speaker and other factors affecting speech intelligibility. *Audiology, 19,* 434–455.

Kaye, J. (1989). *Phonology: A cognitive view.* Hillsdale, New Jersey: Lawrence Erlbaum.

Kimball, J. P. (1973). Seven principles of surface structure parsing in natural language. *Cognition, 2,* 15–47.

Kučera, H., & Francis, W. (1967). *Computational analysis of present-day American English.* Providence, RI: Brown University Press.

Labov, W. (1994). *Principles of linguistic change 1: Internal factors.* Oxford, UK: Blackwell.

Lehiste, I. (1970). *Suprasegmentals.* Cambridge, MA: M.I.T. Press.

Lively, S. E., Pisoni, D. B., & Goldinger, S. D. (1994). Spoken word recognition: Research and theory. In M. A. Gernsbacher (Ed.), *Handbook of psycholinguistics* (pp. 265–301). San Diego: Academic Press.

Lukatela, G., Gligorijevic, R., Kostic, A., Savic, M., & Turvey, M. T. (1978). Lexical decision for inflected nouns. *Language and Speech, 21,* 166–173.

Lukatela, G., Gligorijevic, R., Kostic, A., & Turvey, M. T. (1980). Representation of inflected nouns in the internal lexicon. *Memory and Cognition, 8,* 415–423.

Marslen-Wilson, W. (Ed.). (1989). *Lexical representation and process.* Cambridge, MA: MIT Press.

Marslen-Wilson, W. & Komisarjevsky Tyler, L. (1980). The temporal structure of spoken language understanding. *Cognition, 8,* 1–71.

Meringer, R. (1908). *Aus dem leben der Sprache; Versprechen, Kindersprache Nachahmungstrieb.* Berlin: B. Behr.

Meringer, R., & Mayer, K. (1895). *Versprechen und Verlesen: Eine Psychologisch-linguisticische Studie.* Stuttgart: G.J. Goschen. Reprinted 1987, Amsterdam: John Benjamins.

Mitchell, D. C. (1994). Sentence parsing. In M. A. Gernsbacher (Ed.), *Handbook of psycholinguistics* (pp. 375–409). San Diego: Academic Press.

Morgan, J. L., & Demuth, K. (Eds.). (1996). *Signal to syntax: Bootstrapping from speech to grammar in early acquisition.* Mahwah, NJ: Lawrence Erlbaum Associates.

Neel, Amy T., Bradlow, A. R. & Pisoni, D. B. (1996/97). Intelligibility of normal speech: II. Analysis of transcription errors. *Research on Speech Perception, Progress Report No. 21.* Bloomington: Indiana University.

Norman, D. A. (1981). Categorization of action slips. *Psychological Review, 88,* 1–15.

Pisoni, D. B. (1981). Some current theoretical issues in speech perception. *Cognition, 10,* 249–259.

Pisoni, D. B., Luce, P. A., & Nusbaum, H. C. (1986). The role of the lexicon in speech perception. *Research on Speech Perception, Progress Report No. 12.* Bloomington: Indiana University.

Remez, R. E., Rubin, P. E., Berns, S. M., Pardo, J. S., Lang, J. M. (1994). On the perceptual organization of speech. *Psychological Review, 101,* 129–156.

Sapir, (1921). *Language.* New York: Harcourt, Brace.

Shillcock, R. (1990). Lexical hypotheses in continuous speech. In Gerry T. M. Altman (Ed.), *Cognitive models of speech processing: Psycholinguistic and computational perspectives* (pp. 24–49). Cambridge, MA: MIT Press.

Shriberg, L. D., & Kent, R. D. (1982). *Clinical phonetics.* New York: Wiley.

Small, L. H., Simon, S. D., & Goldberg, J. S. (1988). Lexical stress and lexical access: Homographs versus nonhomographs. *Perception and Psychophysics, 44,* 272–280.

Tanenhaus, M. K., Leiman, J. M., & Seidenberg, M. S., (1979). Evidence for multiple stages in the processing of ambiguous words in syntactic context. *Journal of Verbal Learning and Verbal Behavior, 18,* 427–441.

Van Ooijen, B. (1996). Vowel mutability and lexical selection in English: Evidence from a word reconstruction task. *Memory and Cognition, 25,* 573–583.

Vihman, M. M. (1981). Phonology and the development of the lexicon: Evidence from children's errors. *Journal of Child Language, 8,* 239–264.

Voss, B. (1984). *Slips of the ear: Investigations into the speech perception behaviour of German speakers of English.* Tübingen, Germany: Gunter Narr Verlag.

Wright, R., Frisch, S. & Pisoni, D. B. (1996/97). Speech perception. *Research on Speech Perception, Progress Report No. 21.* Bloomington: Indiana University.

Zwicky, A. M. (1979). Classical malapropisms. *Language Sciences, 1,* 339–348.

Zwicky, A. M. (1982). Classical malapropisms and the creation of a mental lexicon. In L. K. Obler & L. Menn (Eds.), *Exceptional language and linguistics* (pp. 115–132). New York: Academic Press.

Zwicky, A. M., & Zwicky, E. D. (1986). Imperfect, puns, markedness, and phonological similarity: With fronds like these, who need anemones? *Folia Linguistica, 3–5,* 493–503.

INDEX